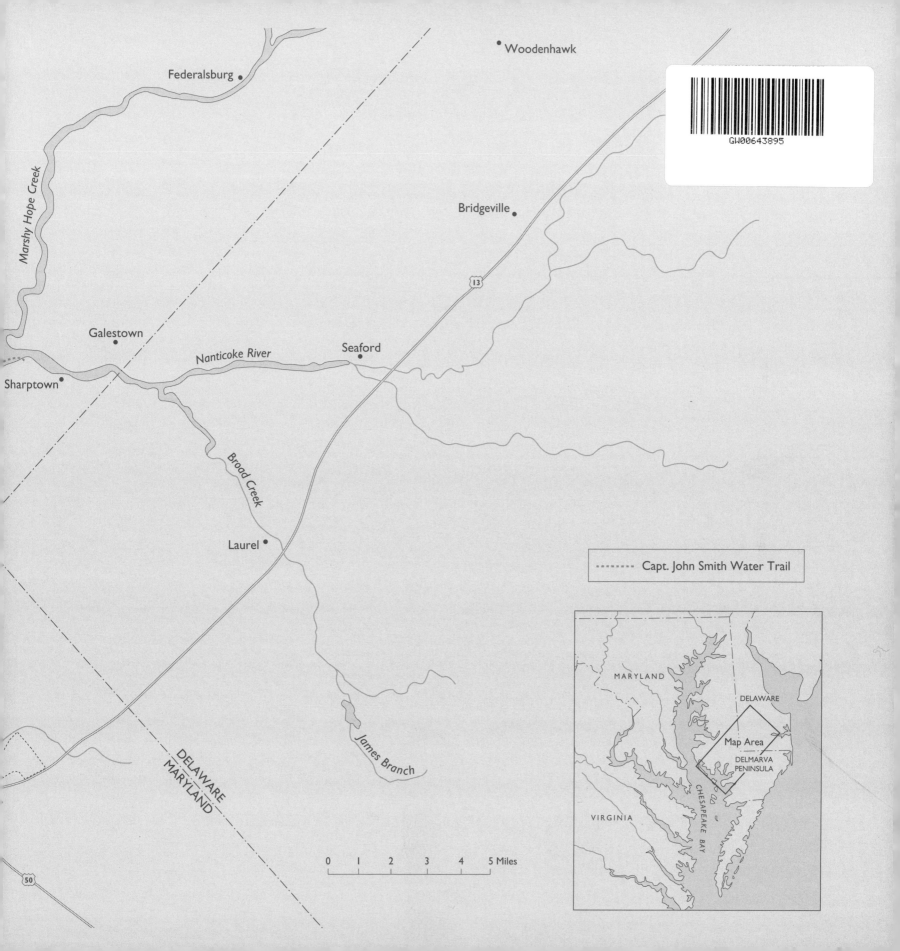

Woodenhawk

Federalsburg

Marshy Hope Creek

Bridgeville

13

Galestown

Nanticoke River

Seaford

Sharptown

Broad Creek

Laurel

DELAWARE
MARYLAND

James Branch

50

-------- Capt. John Smith Water Trail

MARYLAND

DELAWARE

Map Area

DELMARVA
PENINSULA

CHESAPEAKE BAY

VIRGINIA

0   1   2   3   4   5 Miles

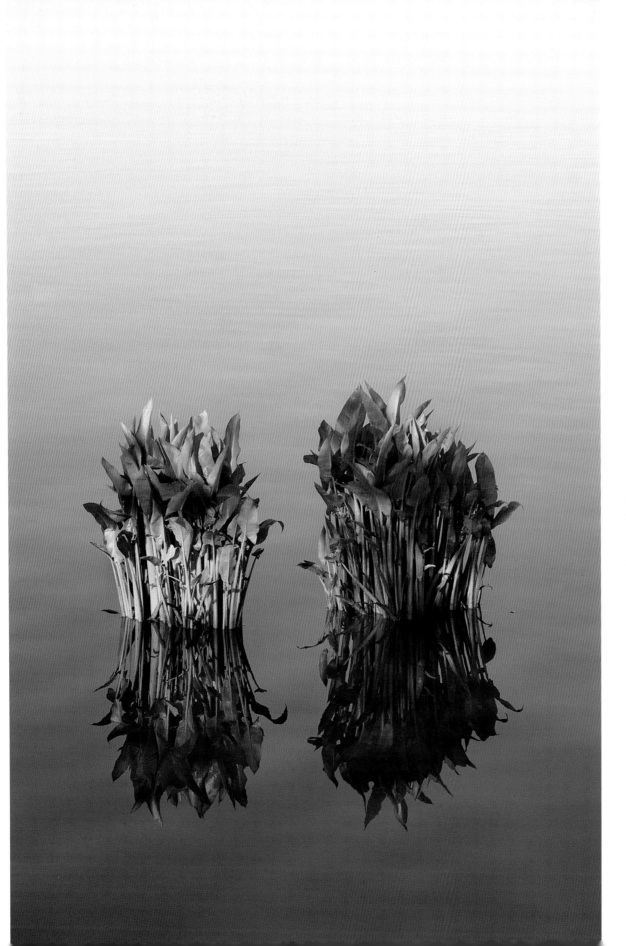

Clumps of pickerelweed
emerge from a tidal flat.
Their starchy tubers were a
staple of the Native American diet.

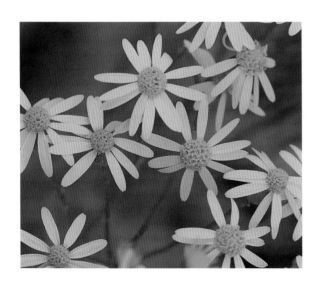 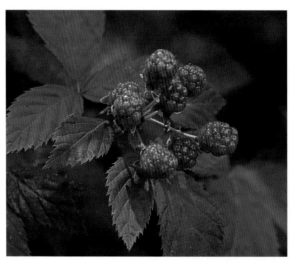

Creek colors—Golden rag-
wort (*far left*) signals May
along the banks of Gales
Creek; blackberries (*left*)
ripen on Big Creek in July.

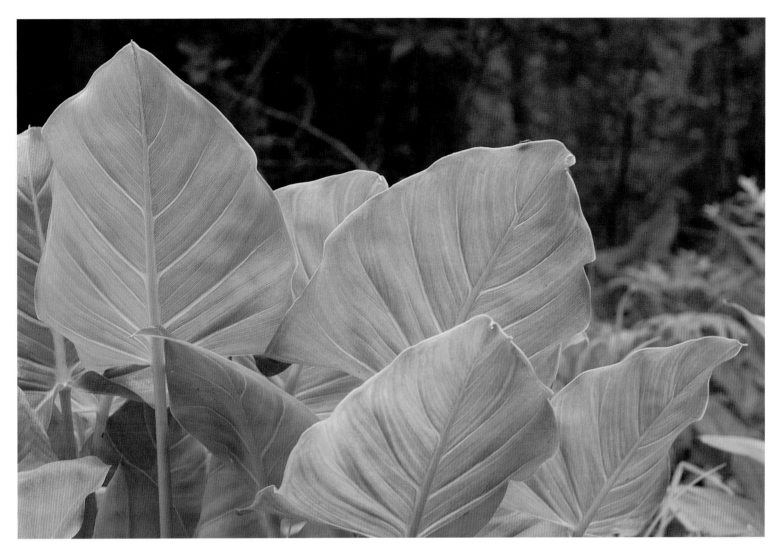

Spatterdock in its fresh May
green. Thick belts of this
aquatic emergent line the
river for miles above Vienna
where the water is fresher.

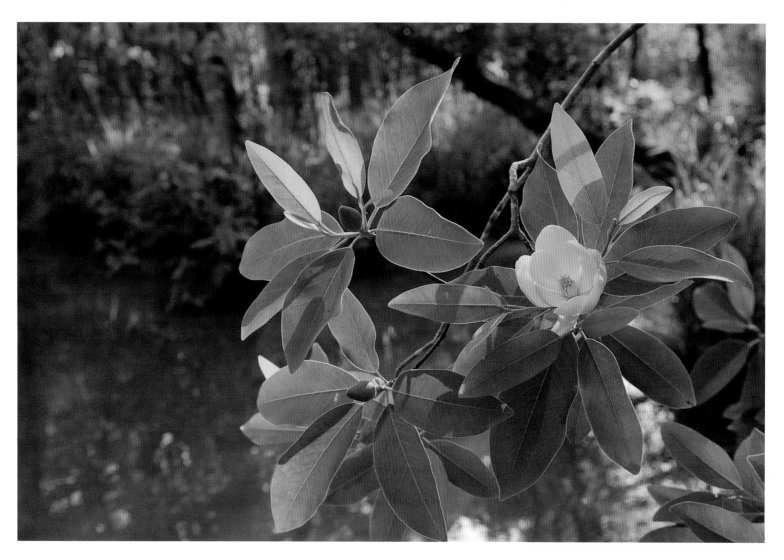

Sweet bay magnolia scents the shores of Big Creek in early June. In autumn its seed cones blush deep red.

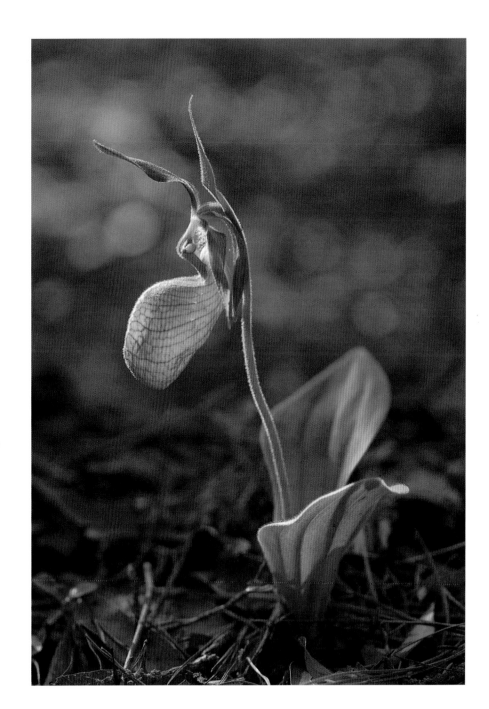

Pink lady slipper, a native orchid, sprouts from an ancient sand dune preserved by the Nature Conservancy.

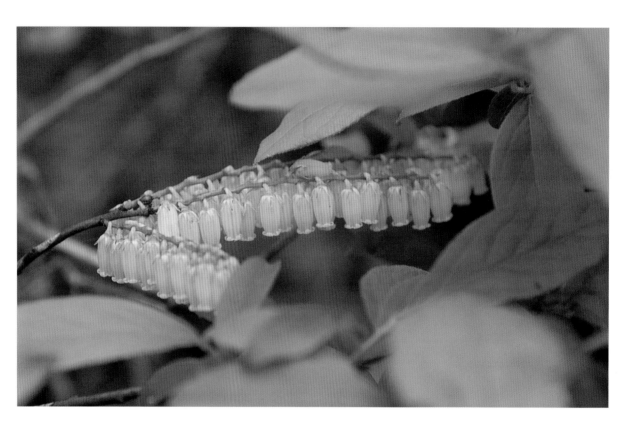

Fetterbush overhangs the
winding forested creeks of
the mid-Nanticoke.

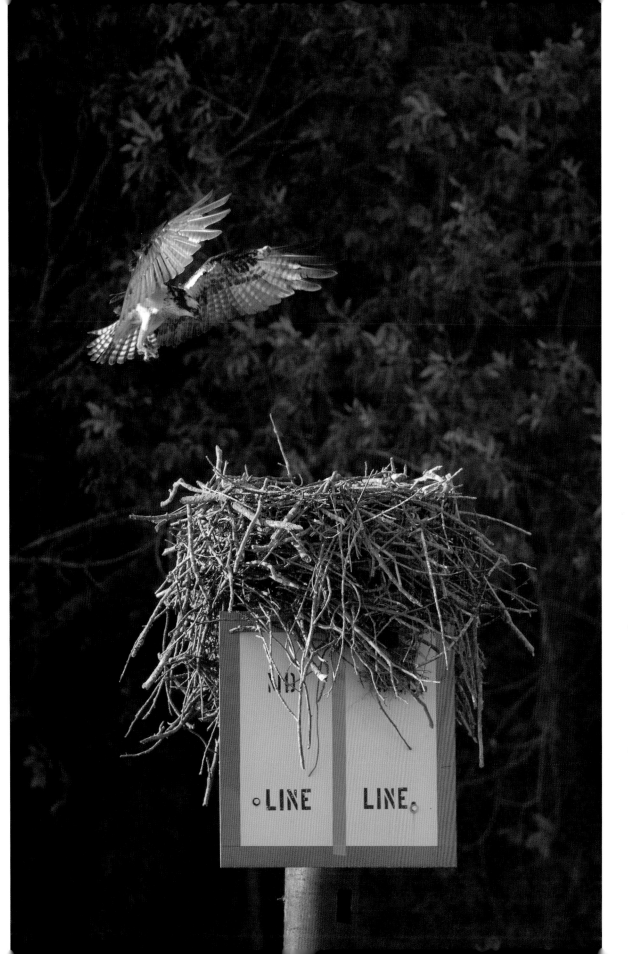

A bi-state osprey returns home on the Maryland-Delaware line marker just north of Sharptown. The river's ospreys arrive around St. Patrick's Day each year from as far south as Belize.

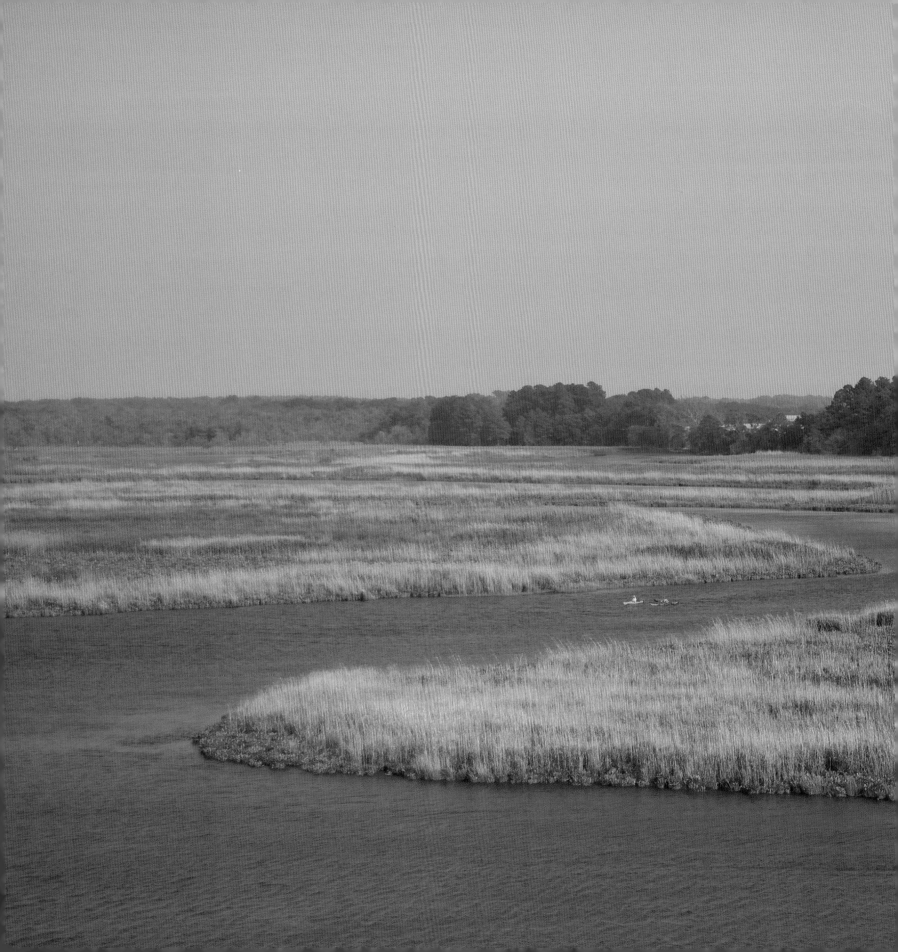

David W. Harp and Tom Horton

THE NANTICOKE

Portrait of a Chesapeake River

THE JOHNS HOPKINS UNIVERSITY PRESS   BALTIMORE

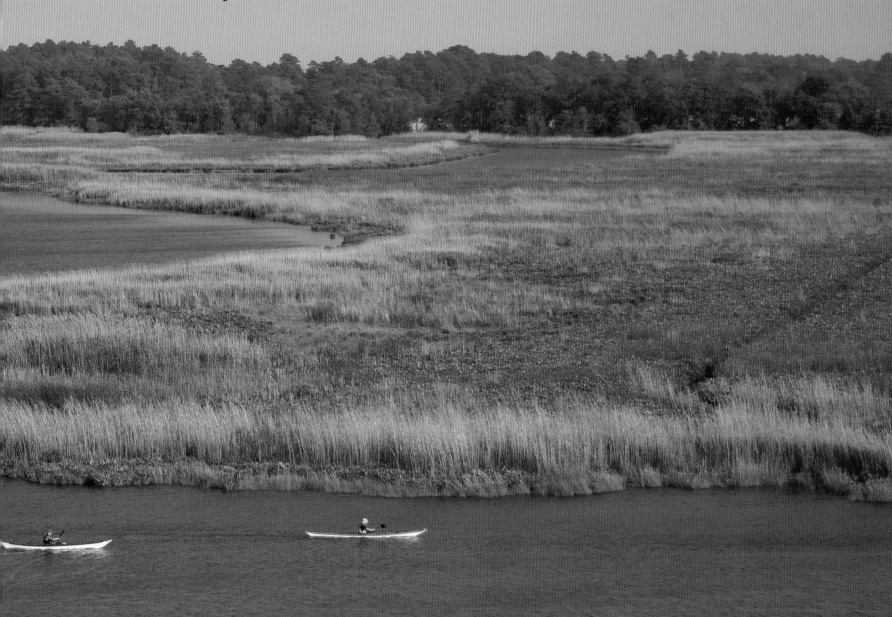

© 2008 The Johns Hopkins University Press
All rights reserved. Published 2008
Printed in China on acid-free paper
9 8 7 6 5 4 3 2 1

The Johns Hopkins University Press
2715 North Charles Street
Baltimore, Maryland 21218-4363
www.press.jhu.edu

Library of Congress Cataloging-in-Publication Data

Harp, David W.

   The Nanticoke : portrait of a Chesapeake river /
David W. Harp and Tom Horton.

      p.   cm.

   ISBN-13: 978-0-8018-9057-4 (hardcover : alk. paper)

   ISBN-10: 0-8018-9057-8 (hardcover : alk. paper)

   1. Natural history—Nanticoke River (Del. and Md.)
2. Natural history—Nanticoke River (Del. and Md.)—
Pictorial works. 3. Nanticoke River (Del. and Md.)
4. Wild and scenic rivers—Nanticoke River (Del. and Md.)
I. Horton, Tom, 1945– II. Title.

   QH104.5.N36H37 2008

   508.752'1—dc22   2008007946

A catalog record for this book is available from the British
Library.

Title page spread: Kayakers weave through the marshes of
Barren Creek on a summer evening.

*Special discounts are available for bulk purchases of this book. For
more information, please contact Special Sales at 410-516-6936 or
specialsales@press.jhu.edu.*

The Johns Hopkins University Press uses environmentally
friendly book materials, including recycled text paper that
is composed of at least 30 percent post-consumer waste,
whenever possible. All of our book papers are acid-free, and
our jackets and covers are printed on paper with recycled
content.

To the late Tom Tyler,

and to the ever watchful Judith Stribling

and Friends of the Nanticoke.

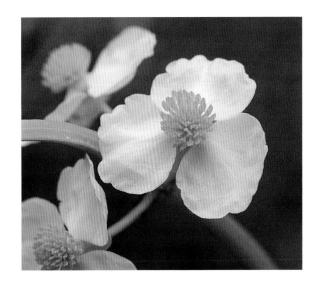

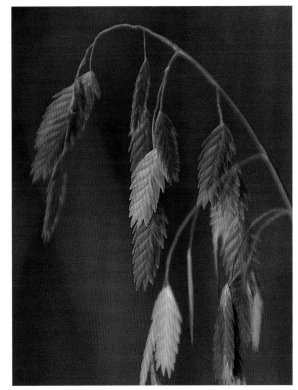

Arrowhead in flower (top); and the rare *Chasmanthium latifolium* (bottom), found only along the Nanticoke in the Delmarva region.

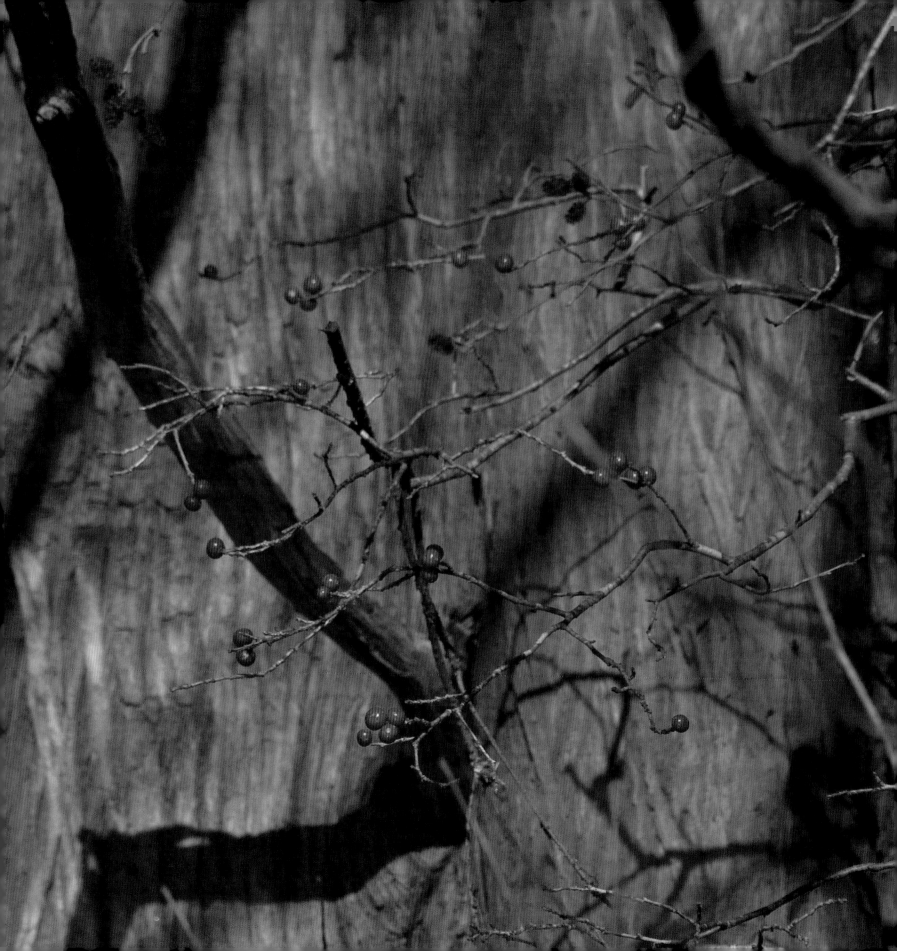

PREFACE

Tools of our trade—notebook and camera, kayak and canoe, a good alarm clock because early light on the river is too precious to miss. Close to a decade living around the Nanticoke for David Harp now—more than half a century for me.

All that time and just this morning, October 12, 2007, I count five different reds for the first time—Virginia creeper, swamp maples, black gum, native viburnum, and winterberry holly—all glowing autumnally as the rising sun hunts through the swamps, flushing out beauty.

We paddle through the white bones of a giant sycamore, reflected perfectly on the still water of a cove. Cold smoke, silver-blue mist warming to gold, steams from the slatey surface. It moves with the river's flow, giving intimate form to every back eddy, whorl, current line, and ripple—a rich calligraphy, invisible most of the time.

I've been doing this nature stuff long enough that I could rise late, go directly to the computer and hack out a creditable enough description of sunrise mornings, fall comes to the Chesapeake, and the like. But Harp can't make it up. He and his lenses must actually be there—and so I tag along and am always rewarded with something new—always—even after fifty years in the out of doors.

You'd think after so long a time around one river a person would have a concise, well-ordered story to tell about what has happened there environmentally. When I was a boy in the 1950s there was plenty of good fishing, crabbing, oystering, and hunting. This despite raw sewage flowing from all the little river towns and gross pollution from tomato canneries, poultry plants, and sand and gravel operations. Ospreys and eagles were getting scarce as DDT spread through the environment.

Opposite: Winter light sets winterberry holly glowing against an old cypress trunk on Broad Creek.

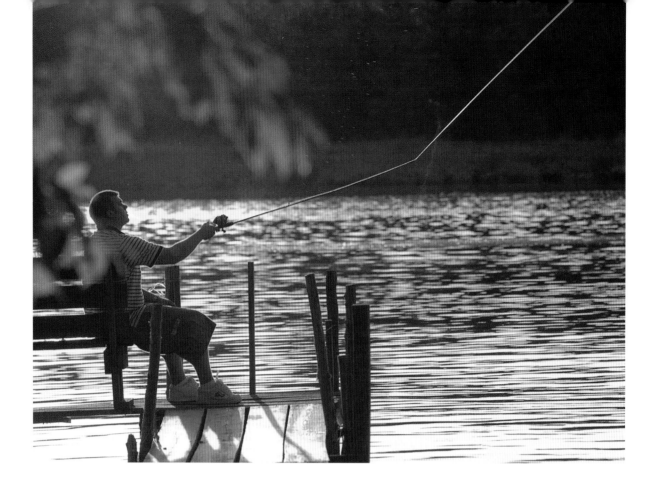

xiv

Casting for white perch off Riverton is a ritual of March and April, when the fish mass to spawn in the tidal freshwater.

Fast forward a few decades and pollution from sewage and industries was dramatically reduced, but pollution from the landscape, runoff from intensive modern farming, from development's paving and tree felling had shot up. Overfishing for rockfish and shad and oysters had also taken a toll. DDT was banned, and eagles and ospreys were coming back.

Nowadays we're at least trying to reduce pollution from all those sources and earnestly regulating fishing pressure—even restocking species like shad and oysters. But the human population, which has more than doubled since I was a boy, continues to grow—and our laws and technologies don't nearly offset the slide toward less nature. Eagles and ospreys meanwhile are more abundant than ever.

Our hope for this book is that it will focus attention on one of the Bay's finest tidal rivers and its watershed; that we can move toward restoring and enhancing the natural environment there, rather than just slowing or halting its decline.

We owe considerable thanks for help in our efforts to more people than we can list here, but especially notable are the following. Generous financial assistance came from Patrick Noonan, Blaine Phillips, Albert Williams, Turney

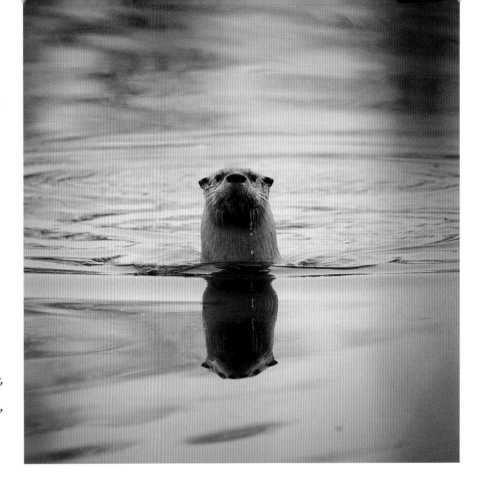

A river otter surfaces in a tidal pond near Eldorado on the Marshy Hope.

Overleaf: Autumn's rich palette warms the edges of Chicone Creek, the old reservation of the Nanticoke Indians.

McKnight, Ned Symes in memory of Anne Patterson Symes and Edward Symes Jr., James Shaw, Keith McMahan, Raymond Nichols, Bill Dennis, and Larry Walton. Special thanks to Neil Kaye, an expert and enthusiastic pilot who provided helicopter time for aerial photography that a project of this sort would normally never dream of. River people who gave generously of their time and knowledge include the farming, fishing Calloway families, watermen Harry and Paula Insley, shad biologist Mike Stangl, Salisbury Towing, and its tugboat Captain Jimmy Hess.

People interested in helping protect the Nanticoke region's water quality, fisheries, and traditional landscapes for forests, farms, and wetlands should contact Friends of the Nanticoke, the Nanticoke Watershed Alliance, the Nature Conservancy's Maryland chapter, and the Conservation Fund in Arlington, Virginia.

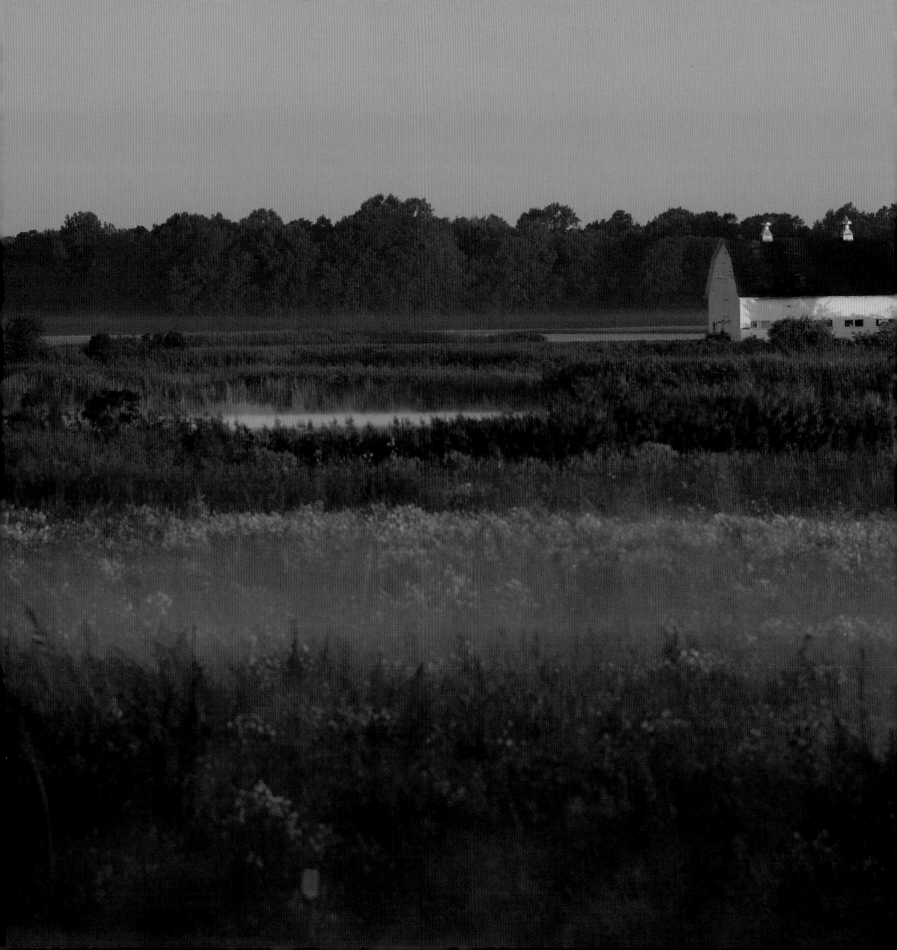

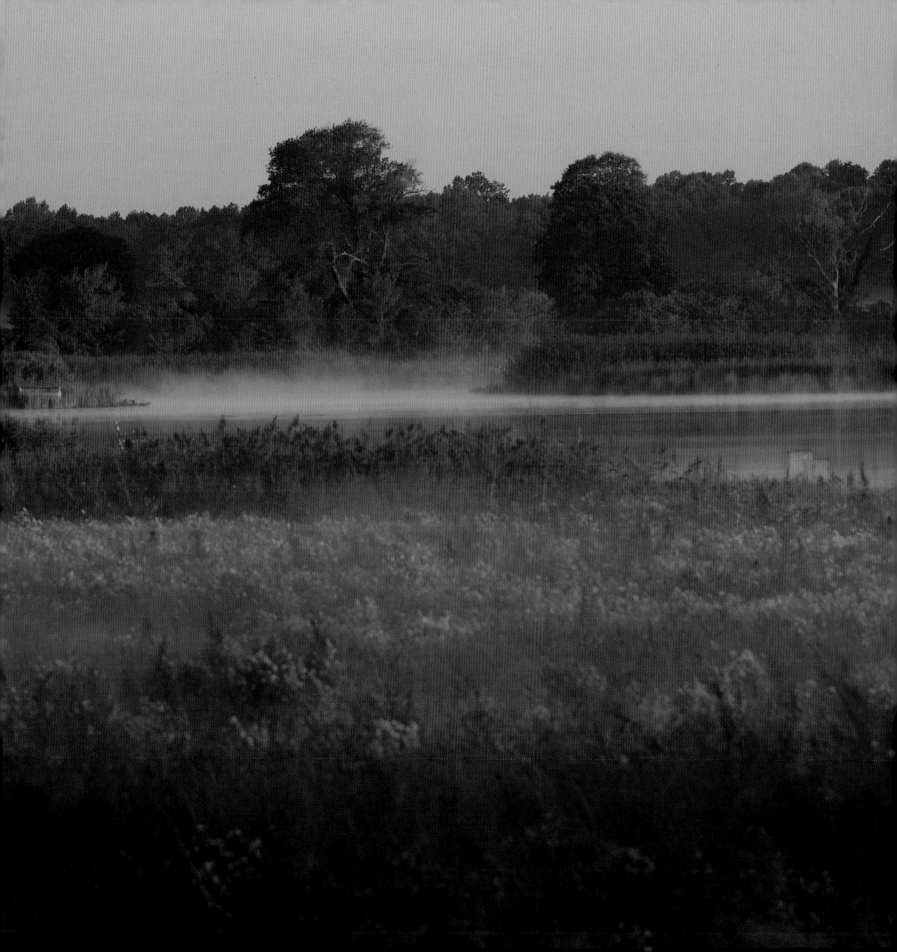

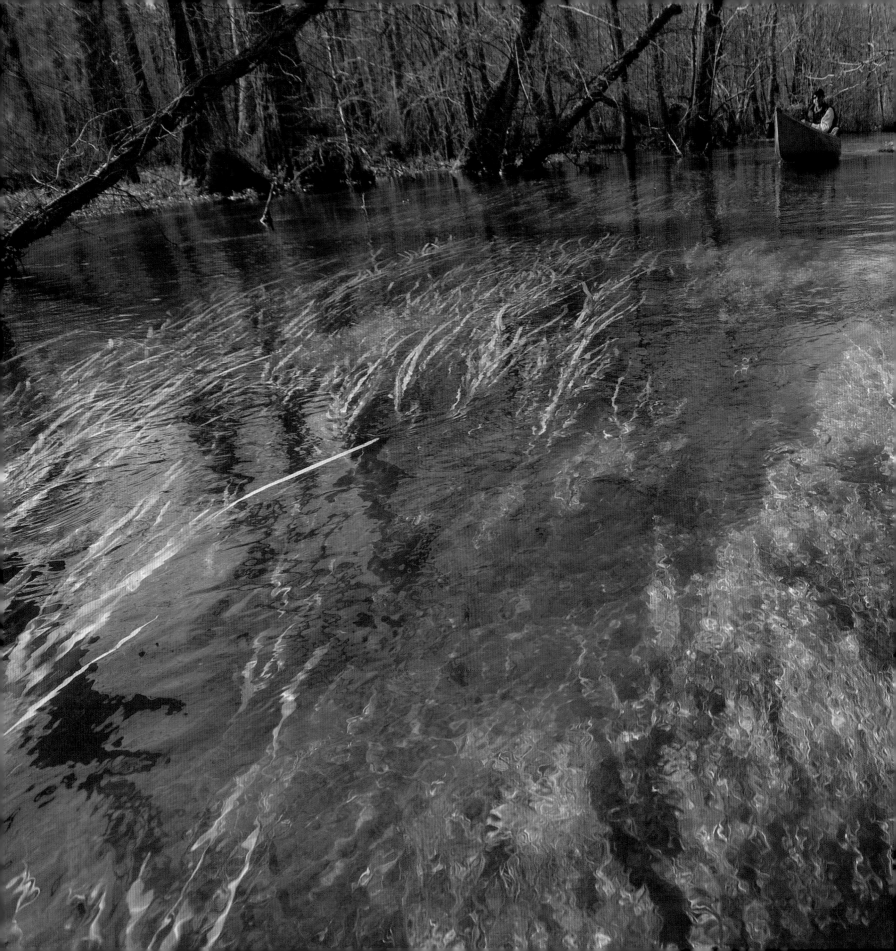

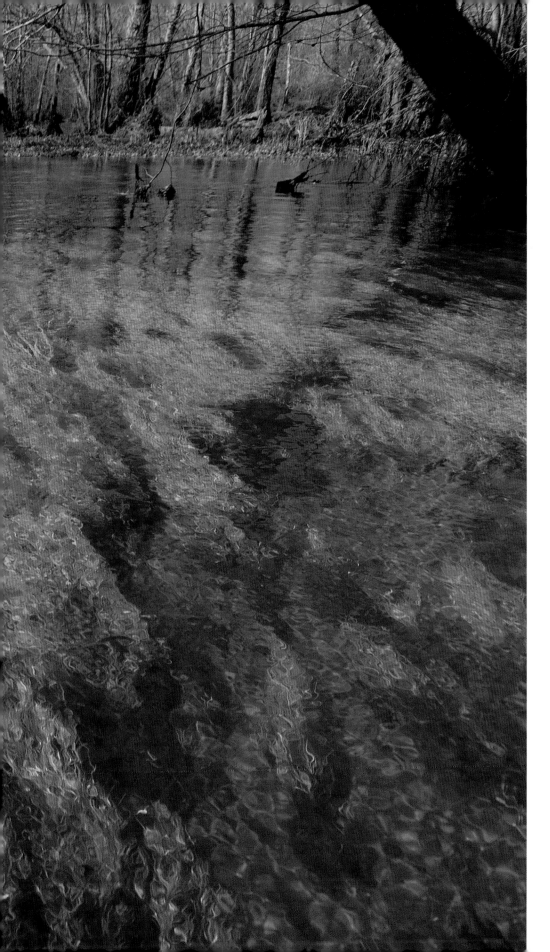

Marshy Hope headwaters:
ribbongrass and callitriche,
spangled with April sun,
thrive in the clear, non-
tidal waters where the river
turns from drainage ditch
to natural stream.

xix

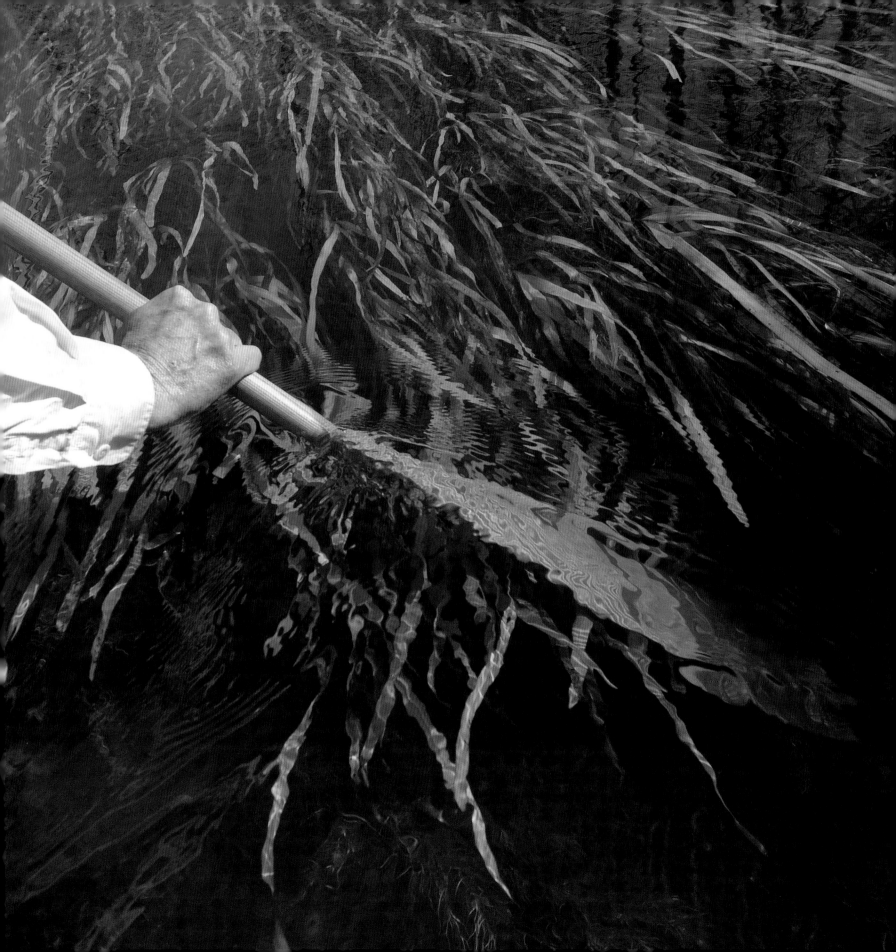

RIVERTOPS

The river, among the wildest and loveliest in the six-state, 64,000-square-mile watershed of Chesapeake Bay, begins as a ditch.

It stretches brown and shallow, arrow straight and boring, treeless banks sculpted by draglines to 45-degree slopes where we plop the canoe in at Route 404 near Woodenhawk in Delaware.

But ditch maintenance ceases not long into our few-mile journey south to Atlanta Road, where Sussex County adjoins Caroline in Maryland. And the universal tendency of free-flowing water to wander, curve, and loop quickly reasserts itself.

Roots and stumps and shrubs roughen the banks now, catching sediments in which little wetlands take root. The flow is forced around these obstacles, bending to and fro, carving channels, twinkling in the sunlight where it burbles over fallen, mossy logs. Overhanging river birches offer pockets of shade, dimpled by minnows, stalked by a great blue heron. A beaver chew blazes freshly on a swamp maple. A big woodpecker, a pileated, flits overhead.

Behind lies the straight line, the river in name only, constructed to perform one vital duty—quickly, smoothly, efficiently draining stormwater off the flat corn and bean fields across the Delmarva Peninsula. Ahead lies meander, complexity, the river serving no one purpose, maximizing no single thing, rather promoting life in all its beauty and diversity.

The forest thickens as the stream spreads into a broad swamp from which shrilling wood ducks erupt, wheep-wheep-wheeping as we pass. The emerging tree leaves of chilly April gauzily filter the morning sun, casting a green-golden light. The sun-infused stream flows clean and clear across sand and gravel, rippling through long, undulating blades of ribbon grass, a submerged aquatic plant. Luxuriant, pillowlike masses of another watergrass, callitriche (Greek for beautiful hair) also

Opposite: Exploring the rivertop, one of several flowing creeks where the Nanticoke and Marshy Hope begin around the edges of a watershed covering more than half a million acres.

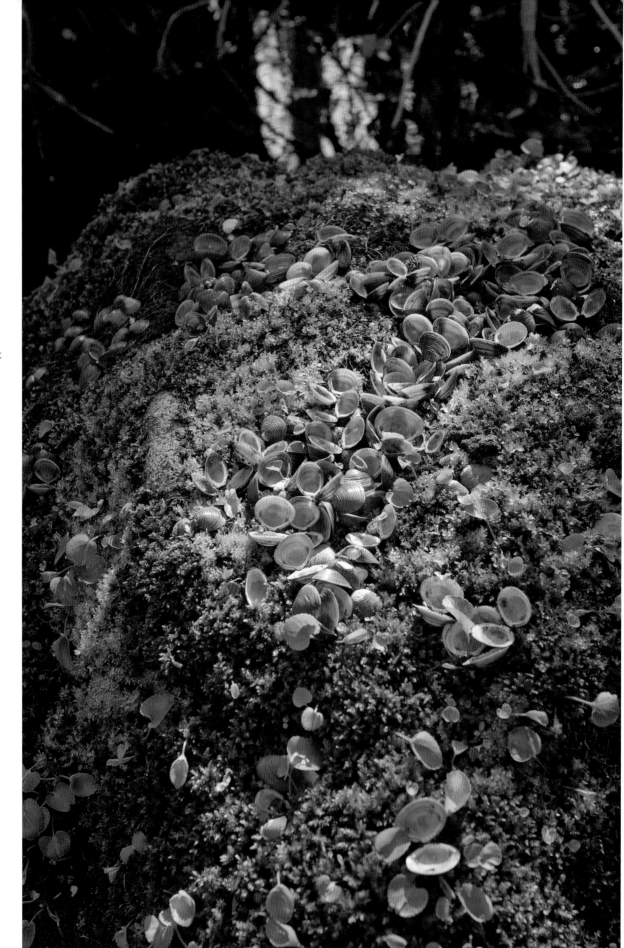

Leavings from an otter feast litter a mossy stump on the upper Marshy Hope.

line the stream, dressing it in the freshest, spring green imaginable.

The river's return to life includes humans too. A rope swing dangles above a deep hole. A small clearing shows signs of foot traffic for several yards along the bank, perhaps netters come to dip spring herring, drawn salmon-like, from the Atlantic to spawn by the scent of where they were born.

Around a bend, the gathering current forces our canoe into a hidden side channel, where a banquet table is set. An old stump in midstream, its top richly upholstered in moss, is piled with little freshwater clams, recently opened and devoured by a river otter, to judge from the scat on a nearby log. Their delicately colored cream and gray interiors are still wet, glistening in the swamplight.

Our chosen route this morning is the upper Marshy Hope Creek. It is just one of many *river-tops*, or beginnings, of the Nanticoke River. They all start as freshwater trickles forty to fifty miles above the river's two-mile wide, salty merge with Tangier Sound and Chesapeake Bay. They fan across a broad arc, roughly bounded by Hurlock, Preston, and Andersontown in Maryland, and Felton, Farmington, Georgetown, and Gumboro in Delaware. They flow down toward Federalsburg in Maryland, and Bridgeville, Seaford, and Laurel in Delaware before enlarging and morphing into arteries of the main river.

The watershed they define—Delaware's largest—drains more than half a million acres of interior Delmarva, the very heart of the great peninsula between Wilmington and Norfolk. It is a region uncelebrated by history books, obscured in public consciousness to this day by Delmarva's famouser fringes—its Atlantic beaches and tidewater shorelines of Chesapeake and Delaware bays.

Opposite: Tender green spring meanders lend color and form to the Nanticoke just above the Delaware line.

The Nanticoke "always was a lonely land, and is so still...its lore scantier than that of any other river," wrote Hulbert Footner in his 1944 classic, *Rivers of the Eastern Shore*. Many of us who grew up there do not see that as a bad thing.

Even Footner never visited the secluded river-tops, navigable only by kayak or canoe, fraught with fallen trees and brushy overhangs that must be pulled over or around, sometimes several times in a mile, places where otters banquet undisturbed, where humans intrude only infrequently.

But those who do are rewarded. Each far-flung finger of the upper Nanticoke has its distinct personality. The James Branch, flowing from Trussum Pond south and east of Laurel, Delaware, requires several hours to navigate a few miles of its deeply forested floodplain. The only other access, bushwhacking in through thickets of greenbrier along the backs of farms, is even more problematic than hauling and shoving the canoe over logs and around blockages dozens of times.

But in midjourney, where the flow broadens and straightens a bit, you enter a realm of giants, one of the extraordinary little pockets of wildness remaining in the mid-Atlantic. A stretch of tea-colored water is sentineled by large bald cypress, a species that makes its northernmost stand in the United States here along the Nanticoke in Sussex County.

"It is a tree so different from any others that it evokes wonder and awe...even a few lend a certain solemnity to otherwise ordinary-looking woodland." So wrote the late John Dennis of Princess Anne, Maryland, in his book *The Great Cypress Swamps*.

Bald cypress are an ancient species of deciduous conifer. Their needles, turning glossy cinnamon before they drop, are a sight to behold in

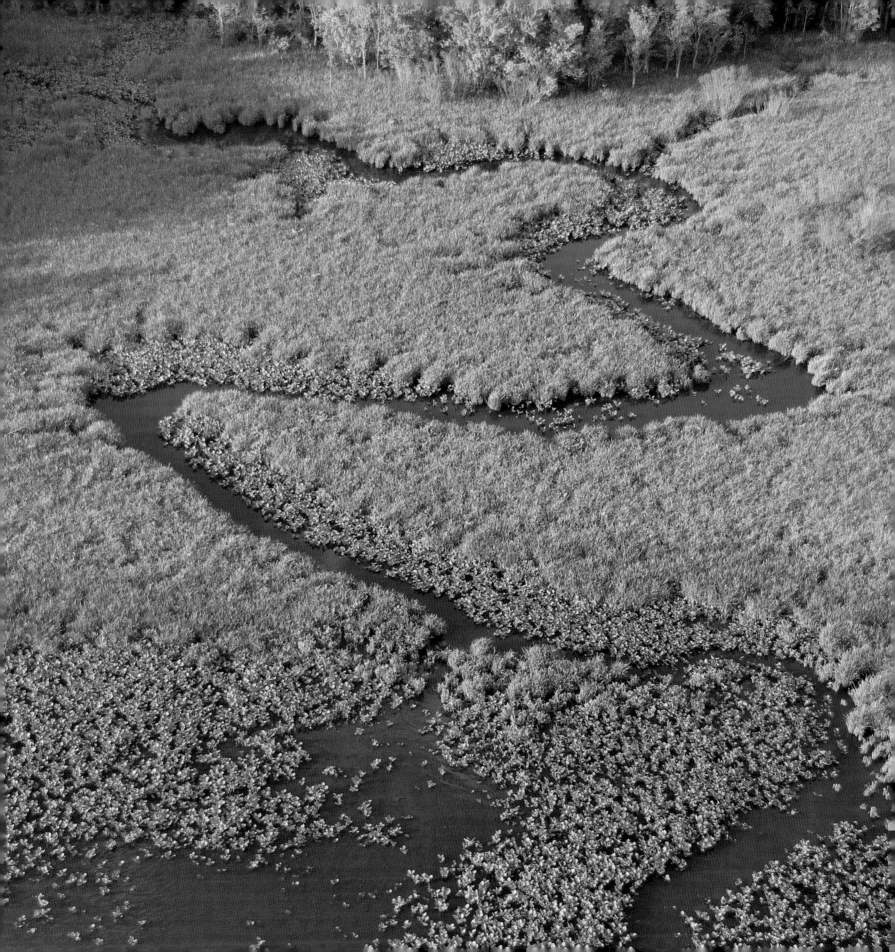

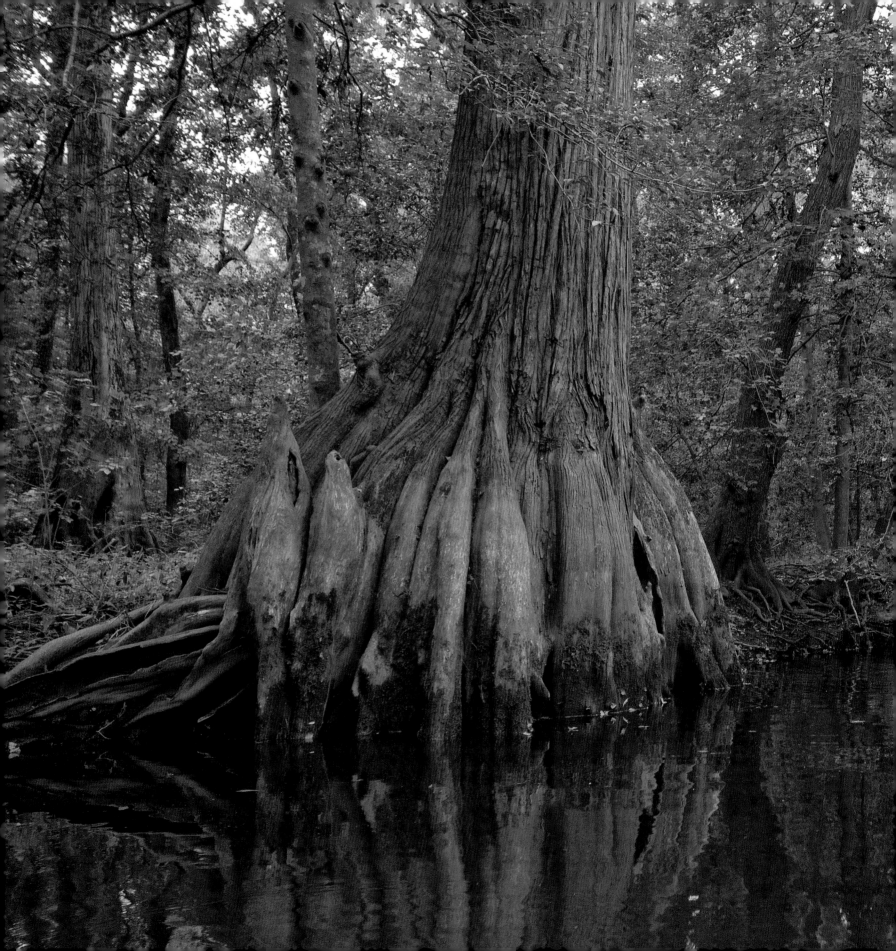

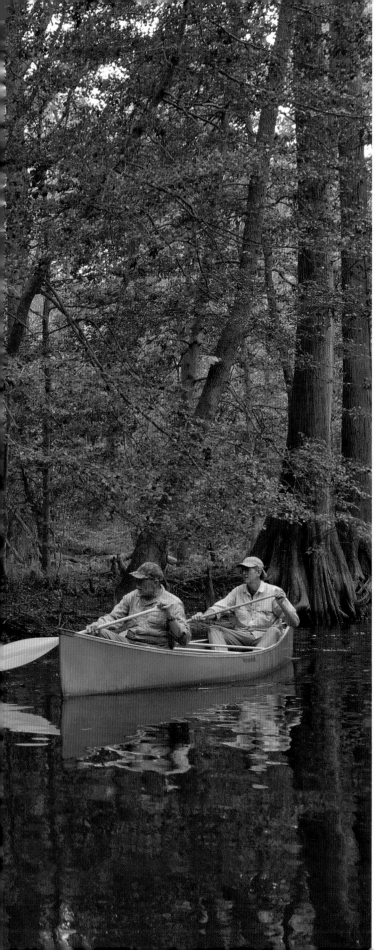

the autumn sun. No other green in the woods is so fresh and airy as that emerging in April and May as the cypress swamp feathers out. The great trees along James Branch somehow escaped the heavy logging nationwide during the eighteenth and nineteenth centuries that felled most of the old cypress for its beautiful wood, both rot resistant and easily worked. A cypress swamp once covered fifty thousand acres on Delmarva in the drainage of an adjacent Eastern Shore river, the Pocomoke.

The largest cypress here, the so-called patriarch, was measured recently at 120 feet in height with a girth of 25 feet. At an estimated 500 years old, it's a child compared with bald cypress elsewhere that have been documented to be well over 1,500 years old—the longest lived trees of any species in the Eastern United States.

Other upstream reaches of the Nanticoke remain rare refuges for another tree species, less im-

James Branch is a refuge of giant old bald cypress, which can live for more than a thousand years. The large base of this tree may indicate that it once grew in more flooded conditions, probably in a millpond whose dam has long gone.

pressive individually than the noble cypress, but collectively a botanical and ecological gem. This is the Atlantic white cedar, so scattered nowadays that the trees are best sought in wintertime, when their dark green needles and ramrod straight trunks stand out from among the leafless maples, gums, and ashes of the freshwater swamps.

Sailors for centuries prized the clear, ale-colored water that flowed from cedar swamps such as once covered thousands of acres around Delmarva. "Tannic and almost medicinal" in taste, "but wondrously soft and pure," wrote Donald Culross Peattie in his 1950 book, *A Natural History of Trees.*

The acidic, peat-tinctured waters, filtered through deep beds of fallen cedar needles, killed the microorganisms that caused even the finest spring water to go foul on long sea voyages. Early American cities also noted the antibiotic properties of the white cedar, boring its rot-resistant logs for pipes in their water systems.

The lightweight, decay-proof lumber from cedars that grew two feet or more in diameter made it a coveted wood for building small boats and shingling homes. Writers remarked on the pleasing resonance of rain striking white cedar shakes, a sound that so impressed one organ maker that he used white cedar for his pipes. The fine charcoal made from white cedar was considered top grade by gunpowder makers among the colonists.

The moist, low-pH environment created by stands of white cedar nurtures other rare, acid-loving species like bog orchids and pitcher plants. Beholding today's scattered cedar clumps around the Nanticoke, one can get only a hint of the dense, brooding swaths that once were a natural wonder of Delmarva.

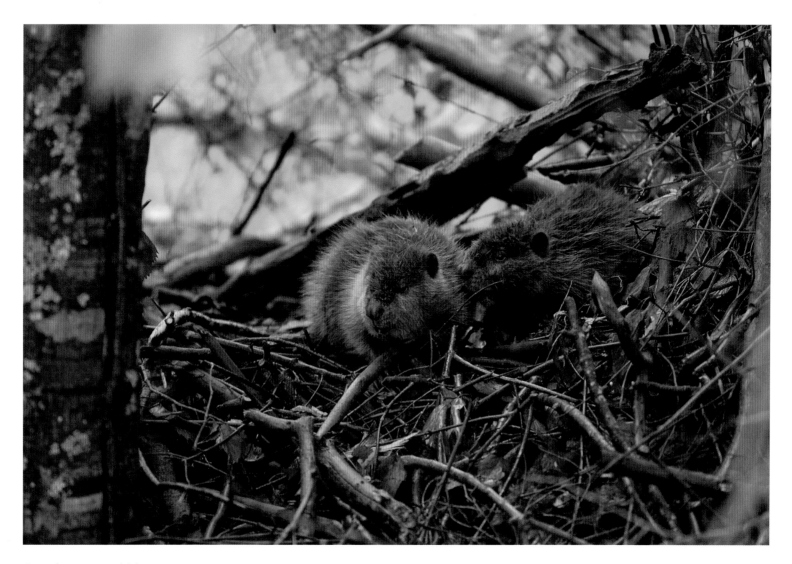

Cute when young—high
water from a tropical storm
has driven these little
beavers from their lodge.
Populations are exploding
along the Nanticoke.

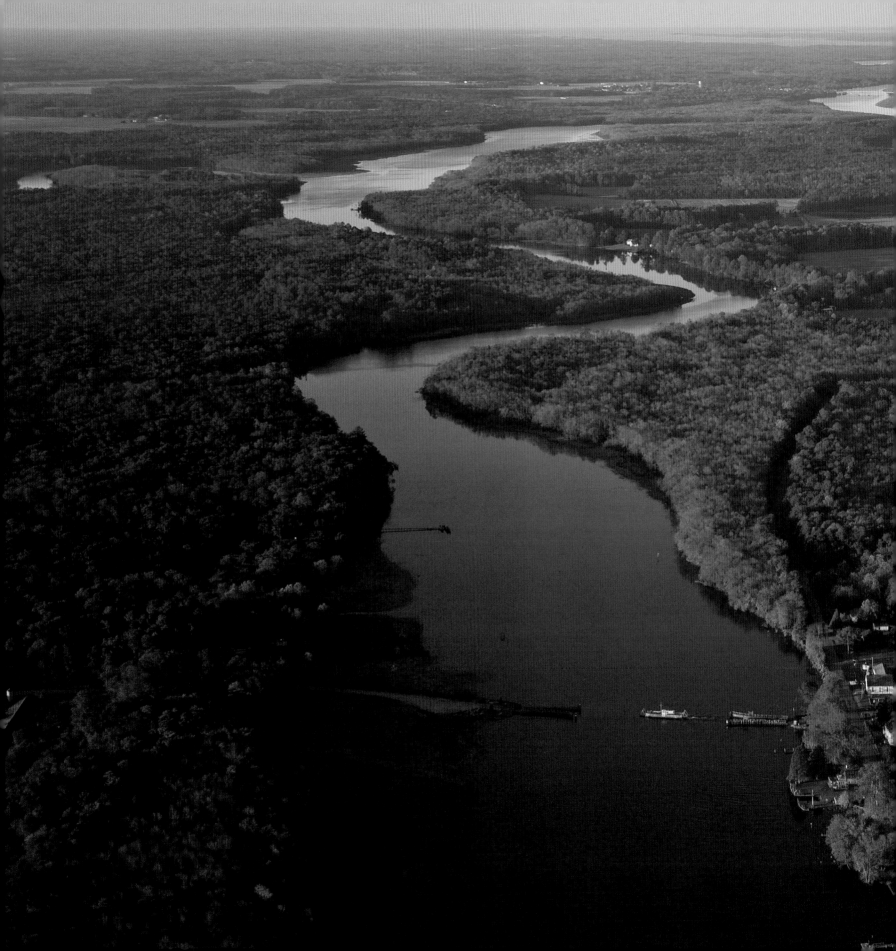

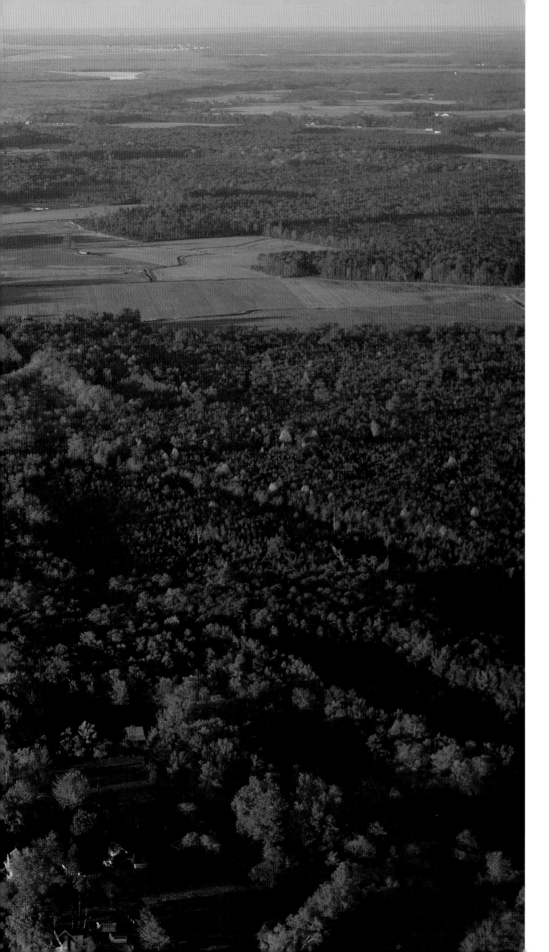

Woodland ferry, looking south toward Sharptown across heavily forested banks, is one of only three such ferries on the Del-marva Peninsula.

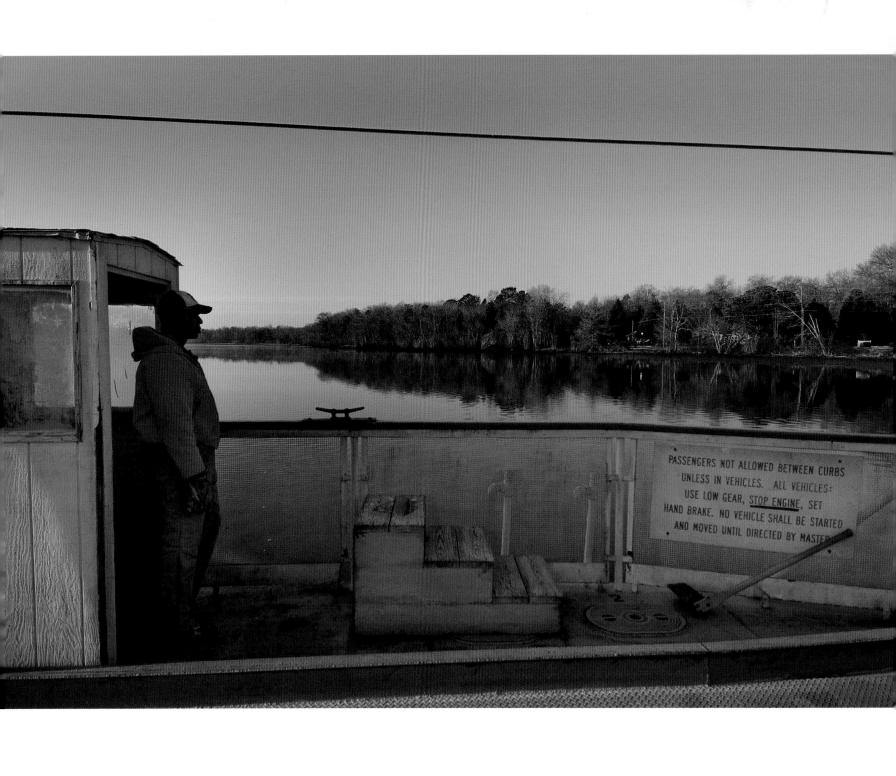

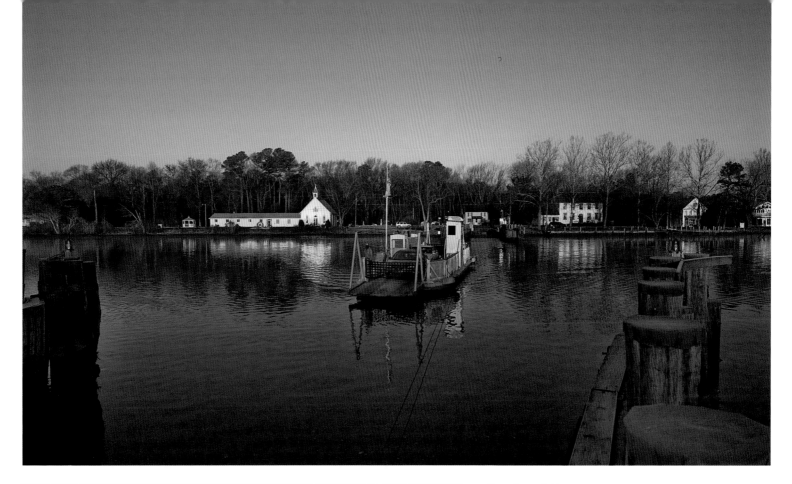

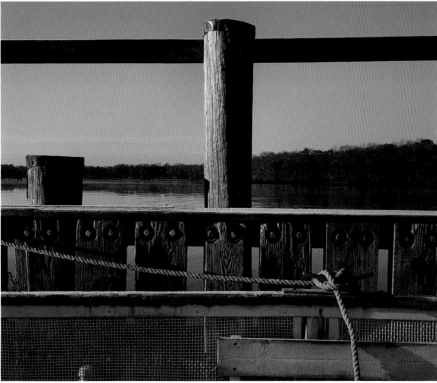

Opposite and this page:
Deckhand Terry Downing
averages 250 trips a day
across the Nanticoke at
Woodland. Fifty thousand
cars a year cross here, the
site of a ferry since the
1670s.

THE CONFLUENCE

By Federalsburg and Seaford the richly branched rivertops have mostly converged to form the two major limbs of the Nanticoke, navigable now by power boats. On rocks and trees in the water you can see the markings of tide, pushing up from the Chesapeake.

Another dozen or so miles downstream and the two main stems join, having also been joined below Seaford by Broad Creek coming from Laurel. There is no formal name for this confluence, but there should be, for if rivers have souls, the Nanticoke's might reside there.

The ancient Greeks had the word *omphalos*, literally meaning navel, also meaning sacred spot, center of the universe, source of mystical power for the Oracle of the famous Temple at Delphi.

The omphalos of the Nanticoke is a great, deep round of tide-swirled water, ringed by forest, one of the sweetest spots in the Chesapeake country. It is where the main Nanticoke sweeps down across the Delaware line into Maryland and swells with its largest tributary, the Marshy Hope, before marching off grandly to the Chesapeake.

It's a place to stop paddling, to cut the engine, to let the eddying currents slowly spin your boat and your view across miles of nearly unbroken woods and rivers going off in three directions as far as the eye can see. Just drift. Watch ospreys and terns dive, herons stalk, eagles circle. Listen to warblers and kingfishers in the woods by day, the hooting of owls by night as a full moon reflects on the rolling of big, cow stripers spawning on the channel edges.

It is easily recognizable on Captain John Smith's 1612 map of the Chesapeake, and there is no reason to think if the good captain returned today, he would find things much different.

There, each in its season, wild rice sends frothy seed heads swaying high above the tidal mudflats,

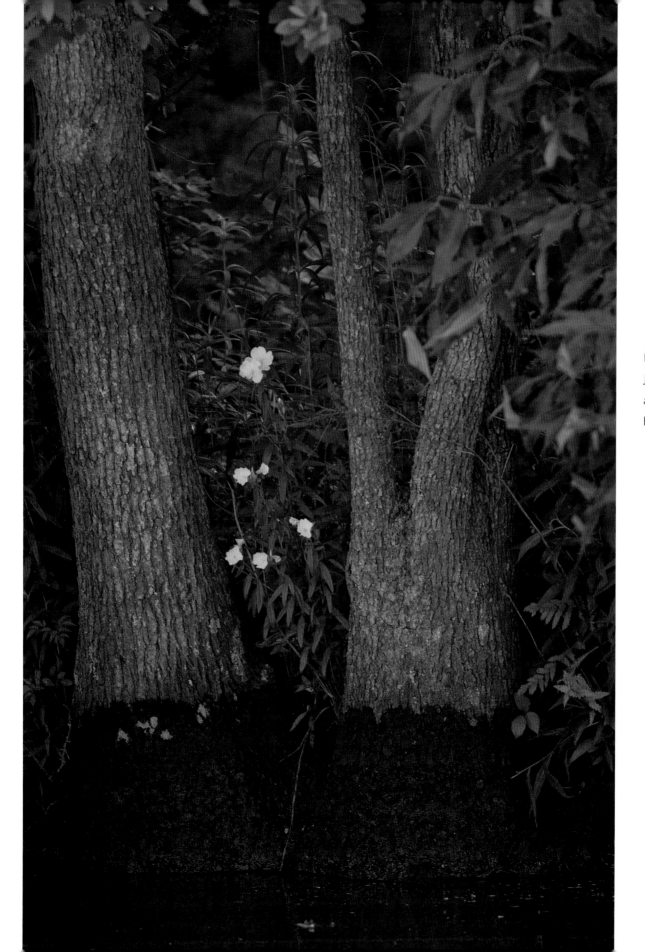

Primrose shines in early
June from the crevices of
a green ash, trunk marked
by tide.

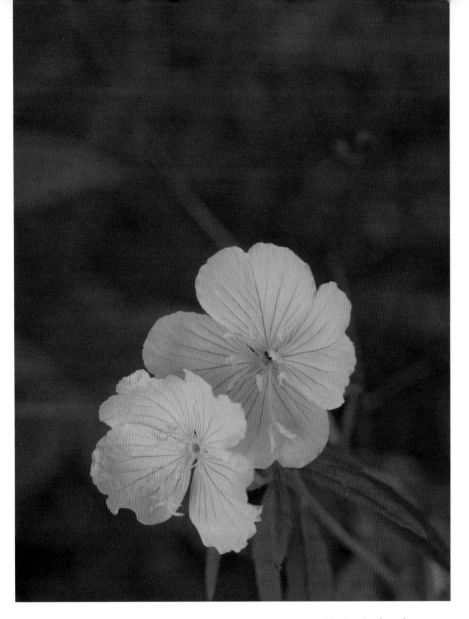

Diminutive but showy, primroses bloom along the dark, wooded edge of Big Creek.

luminous and green-golden; cardinal flower and swamp iris blossom from shaded nooks of the swamp edge; red maples blush and sweetbay magnolia scents the air. Between water and woods lie thick, green belts of spatterdock, arrow arum, pickerelweed, hibiscus, and other aquatic plants beloved by waterfowl, sheltering to the young of fish.

The forested swamps are thickest here, and paddlers may lose themselves for hours in tree-canopied tidal creeks that wind for miles above and below the confluence. There, snapping turtles haul out onto the banks to lay their eggs, and inquisitive river otters in the spring approach within paddle's length. At dusk wild turkeys perch in trees along the edge.

An oddity amid the maze of meandering creeks is a canal not far below the confluence on the western bank, maybe sixty feet across and running straight for more than half a mile back

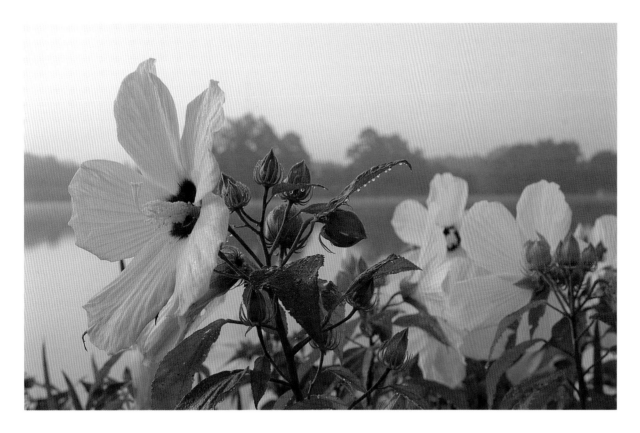

Hibiscus festoons the river's banks through July and August.

into the forest. At its head, where it joins a natural creek, you can see where it once continued some distance more toward high ground but is now choked with sediment and trees. Its origins are a mystery, unchronicled like so much of the Nanticoke's history.

Some claim it was dug by slaves in colonial times, to take produce downriver from Dorchester county farms. Indeed, the canal's filled-in head runs close to Handsell, the shell of a 1700s brick manor home along Indiantown Road just north of Vienna; but roads sufficient to move farm products existed by the 1600s. Possibly the canal was dynamited later in the nineteenth century to float out large white oak timber that grew there.

Locals call these water-woods of the middle-Nanticoke "cripples." The term's origin is murky. An early settler's property deed differentiates among swamps, woods, meadows, marshes, and cripples. Did settlers think it crippled land, impossible to drain and unfit to farm or pasture livestock? The treacherous footing could cripple a cow or a careless human who wandered there.

An Appalachian fiddle tune is called "Cripple Creek," but the only Cripple Creek is a mining town in Colorado. The dictionary offers Old English *crypel* or *croepel* as meaning wet, thickety places, also meaning to creep, to move slowly.

These days we see no impairment, rather virtue in such places; we celebrate the cripples and other wetlands for filtering and absorbing pollutants and for harboring an astonishing array of plants and animals, including many rare ones.

Unique to the Nanticoke, its wetlands are interspersed for many miles upstream and down from the confluence with another striking natural feature: ancient sand dunes, now mostly cloaked in forest, sculpted by winds in the colder, drier climate of the last ice age some twelve thousand years ago. These abundant juxtapositions of soil going from desert to wet and back, and topography shifting rapidly from hill to swamp to hill, create an astounding variety of special habitats.

Most special of all are a handful of easily overlooked shallow, unforested depressions in the landscape known as Carolina bays. Their unique hydrology and soils harbor some of the peninsula's rarest plants and a host of amphib-ians and insects. Their origins are still a matter of debate. Whimsically, old timers tabbed them "whale wallows," presumably formed by the last writhings of leviathans stranded as Noah's biblical flood receded.

Beginning in the 1970s, biological surveys began pointing out the Nanticoke system as something special, eventually documenting it as home to nearly three hundred rare or threatened species of plant and animal—some found in few other places on earth.

In 1991 the Nature Conservancy, the nation's premier conservator of natural lands, designated the river part of a national campaign to preserve last great places. "One of the most pristine and ecologically significant major watersheds in the mid-Atlantic," they wrote.

Wayne Klockner, a Nature Conservancy official, recalls summoning courage in 1995 to bid at auction for the Maryland chapter of the

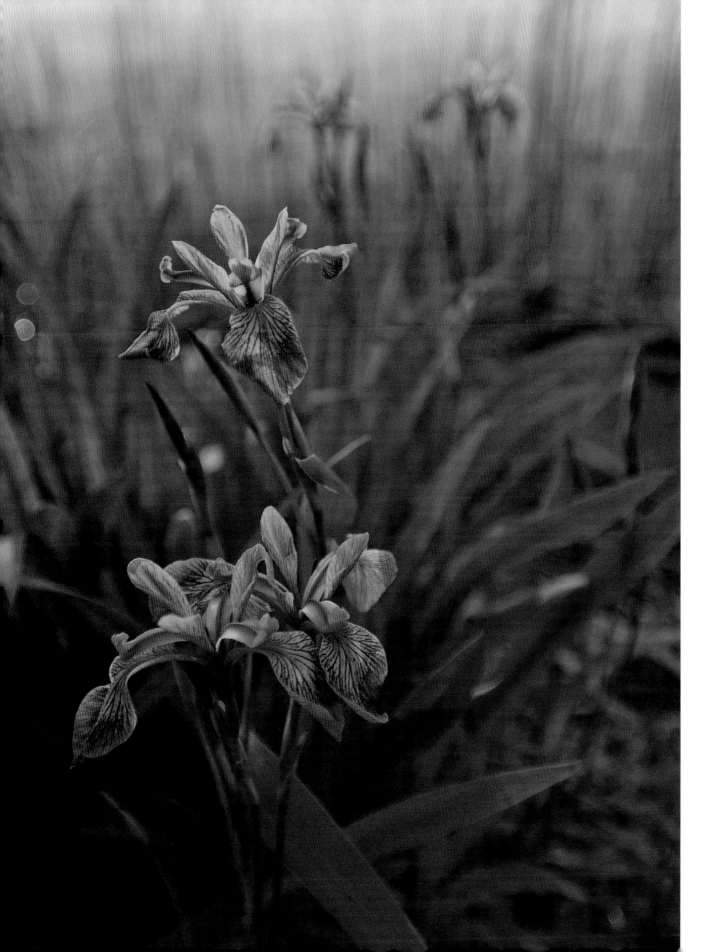

Wild iris pops up along the tidal edge in mid-May.

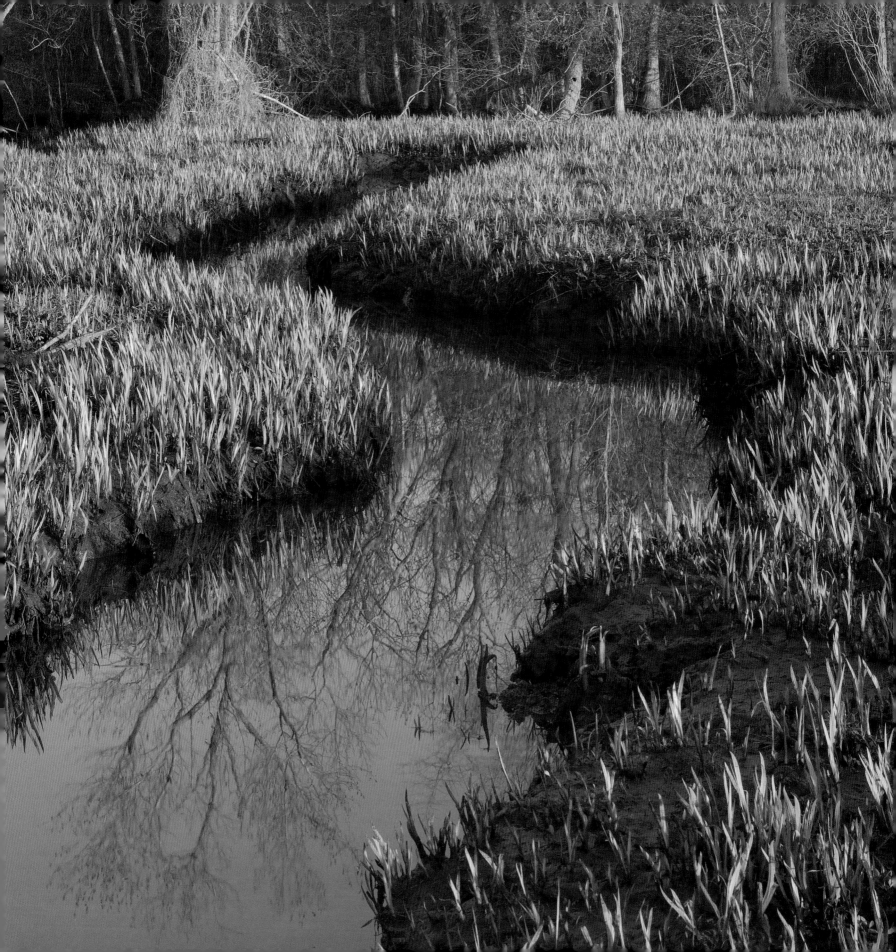

Conservancy's first major purchase along the river, sixty-five waterfront acres in sight of the confluence: "'Do we go to the wall to get this,' I was thinking as the sale started? Just then an eagle flew over—'*yes!*'"

With sprawl development running unchecked across Delmarva, a number of local and national organizations began strategizing to protect the Nanticoke. One didn't have to be versed in biodiversity or the rare Indian sea oat and the silver-bordered fritillary (a butterfly) to see the importance of it. There were so few places left in the growing megalopolis between New York and Richmond where one could fish and hunt, birdwatch, paddle, and waterski along so many miles of unbroken forested beauty.

There was talk of a national park, of state wildlands, of a federal wild and scenic river designation. But in rural Delaware and Maryland, such talk was akin to throwing gasoline on hot coals—the hot coals being strong-held local notions of private property owners' right to do as they pleased with their land.

Enter one Thomas Tyler, to whom this book is dedicated, who represented the biggest private property owner on the river—one of the biggest in the whole, six-state Chesapeake Bay watershed. Tom was regional manager for Chesapeake Forest Products, which owned and managed some five hundred square miles of commercial timberland, including tens of thousands of acres and mile after mile of undeveloped shoreline in the Nanticoke basin.

The company's parent corporation also had an increasingly aggressive real estate development division that believed forestry could no longer compete economically with waterfront lots. Green or paved, the future of the Nanticoke clearly would have a lot to do with Chesapeake.

Opposite: Red maple buds reflect amid the early April marshes. *Acer rubrum* provides some of the year's earliest color, first beginning to blush when hard winter still rules.

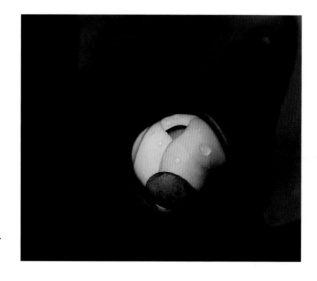

Spatterdock lilies always look as if they are about to blossom gloriously, but this is about it. Snapping turtles eat these delectable flowers.

"Not the slightest doubt—Tom Tyler is going to f—— us," say notes I jotted in December 1993 after a first meeting when we went for beers at the Nanticoke Inn in Vienna.

Tom was raging. He pointed to a friend at the bar whose parents "were told they couldn't thin some pines on their property because of an endangered species on their land…They never even told them what it was and her dad died never knowing." Tom had been to a meeting with environmentalists on the river's future where "this s.o.b., a Rhodes scholar they said, just humiliated me, made me feel about this high."

With a sinking feeling, I feared our Rhodes

scholar might have won a battle and blown the war. Tom's local "cred" went well beyond the commercial forest community. He was an umpteenth generation Eastern Shoreman who had the respect and ear of farmers, local politicians, and rural citizens along the length of the Nanticoke. It wouldn't have taken him more than a few phone calls to foment an instant property-rights uprising against the likes of the Nature Conservancy, the National Park Service, and our local Friends of the Nanticoke environmental group. Right or wrong wouldn't matter. We'd spend years digging out from under the ensuing firestorm.

But there was more to Tom Tyler than that. We'd learn in the next few years that while he could rant with the best of the anti-environment crowd (he took anger-management classes) no one loved the Nanticoke more; and no one was struggling harder to find accommodation between protecting the region's nature and respect-

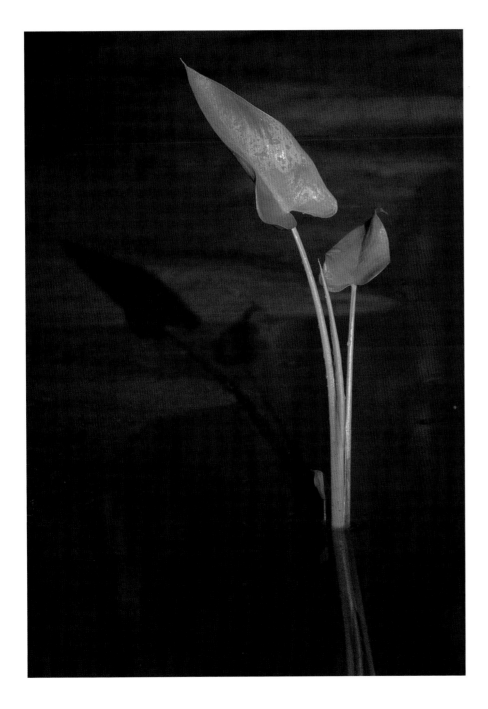

Arrow arum, another plant
important to the nutrition
of Native Americans, arrows
up from the rich silt of
river's edge.

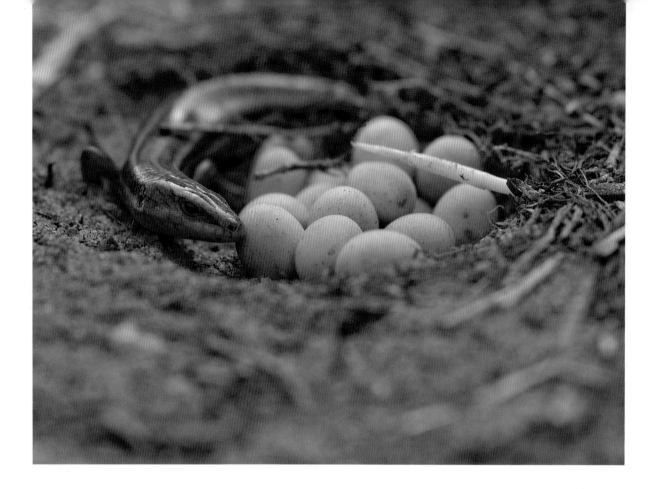

A broadnosed skink tends its eggs on one of the sand dunes characteristic of the Nanticoke's banks.

ing those who made their home and their living there.

Tom would be going on about anti-hunters and the right to bear arms, and then: "I worry a lot that there's not a place left on this river where a duck can rest anymore without being shot at . . . it's a damn shame."

He would pepper me and others like Don Baugh of the Chesapeake Bay Foundation with questions about the environmental community: where was so and so coming from? Did this person really speak for his organization? Did we trust them? What was the real agenda of this or that group?

He'd take anyone who would come on a tour of his sprawling woodlands, showing us the latest in environmentally sensitive harvesting techniques. He'd make no bones about how clear-cuts looked to most of the public: "ugly as hell . . . like rape.

"But you know, we replant and they grow back—and as long as we're making a buck off these lands, they aren't going into development, which is spreading like a damn cancer."

Tom often said he was proud of how the Chesapeake company cut trees, but he purely loved showing off all the lands around the Nanticoke and Delmarva "that we don't cut." That included some breathtaking acreage, old cypress, Atlantic

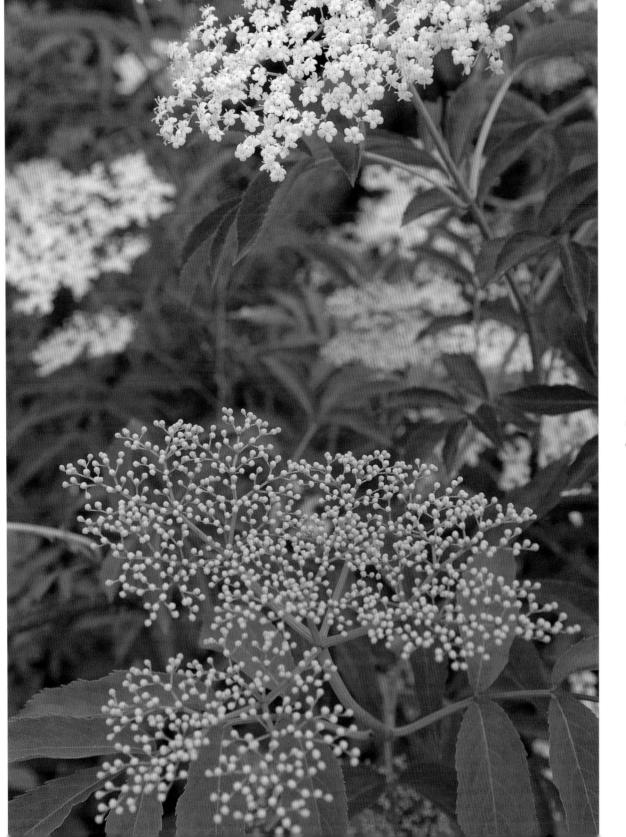

Lacy blooms of water parsnip signal June along the edges of tidal creeks.

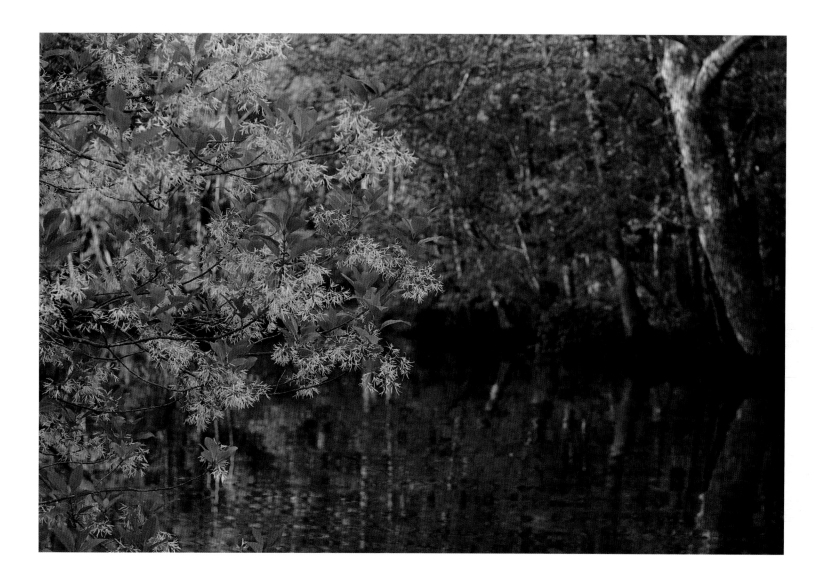

Fringe tree is among the gaudiest and sweetest bloomers along Gales Creek each spring. In autumn it bears purple fruits in clusters.

white cedars, miles of tidal shoreline. "Don't the woods just smell good?" he'd say as we pushed through thickets of southern bayberry and among pine, laurel, magnolia, and cedar.

Tom began spending time laying out canoeing and nature trails along the river with environmental groups, providing camping sites for environmental education trips, lining up heavy equipment for river cleanups, helping organize

the Nanticoke's first annual festival dedicated to restoring the river's overfished shad. I learned later that he endured a lot of criticism and lost some friendships with cronies who thought he was selling out, but he never talked about that to us.

"You still want it all in old growth forest, don't you?" he asked me one day. In a perfect world, yes—the sound of a chain saw along the river

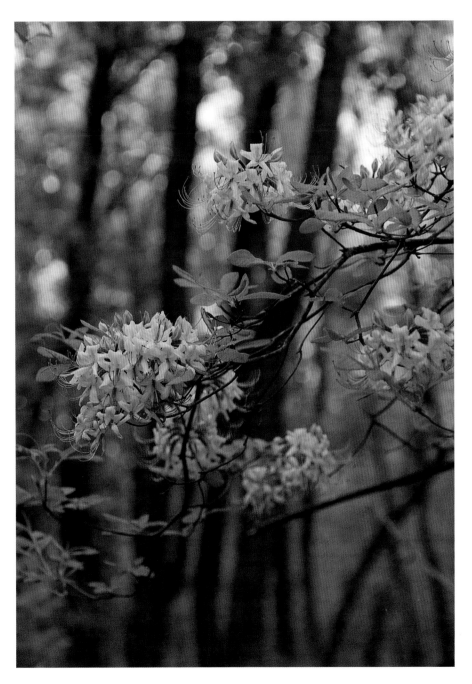

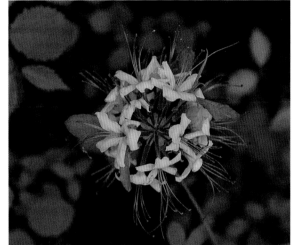

Pink azalea blossoms in early May among the cripples, as the Nanticoke's wooded tidal swamps are called. Origins of the term are obscure, but it may mean slow flowing waters.

28

Golden club grows just
below the millpond dam
at Galestown, a rare occur-
rence. The Nanticoke is a
hotbed of biodiversity in
the Chesapeake region.

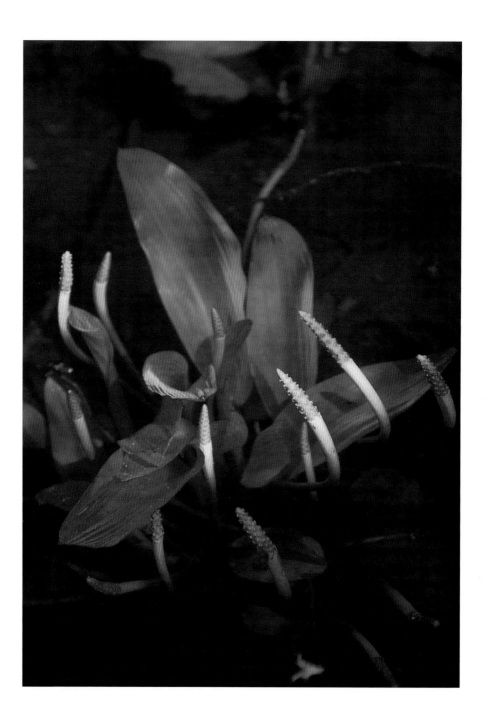

could still spoil my day, I replied. "Where the hell you think that paper you're scribbling on comes from?" he shot back. By then, we could joke like that.

If I could have one wish for the Nanticoke, other than its permanent protection from unwise development, it would be to have Tom still around—delighting in making early morning calls from his truck to wake up various "greenies," inviting you to sample sausage sandwiches with him at diners and country stores along the peninsula, smoking way too much.

But lung cancer, discovered one winter, took him so hard and quick it seemed there was scarcely time for a proper good-bye. He died in the summer of 1996. He was only 55. Hundreds came to his memorial service, from every point of the rural-urban, liberal-conservative, preservationist-property rights compass.

No one imagined it then, but Tom's efforts had helped set in motion a huge payoff for the river.

In June 1999 a complex negotiation concluded that would protect forever from development an astounding 76,000 acres of Chesapeake Forest Products land—more than a hundred square miles—across the Nanticoke basin and other parts of Delmarva. The lands, transferred to state ownership in Maryland, Delaware, and Virginia, would support a mix of uses including commercial forestry, public hunting, and wildlife preservation.

Of that mammoth tract, a personal favorite is a little corner just north of the U.S. 50 bridge off Old Bradley Road on the Wicomico County bank of the Nanticoke: the Tom Tyler Demonstration Forest and Nature Trail, 455 acres of trails and commercial timberland. It contains some of the river's finest Atlantic white cedar. Tom was certain the spot had been a favored haunt of Native Americans.

The acquisition is formally known as the Chesapeake Forest, and you will see small signs designating it across mile after mile of roads on the Peninsula. The 58,000 acres protected in Maryland amounted to 1 percent of the state's entire land surface.

Upstream of the confluence, along the Marshy Hope, the forested corridor provides a nightly resting place for more than a thousand wintering tundra swans that fly here all the way from Alaska's North Slope every autumn. From a secluded logging road screened from the river by tall trees, you can listen to flight after flight of swans settle in on the river around dusk, the din of their wild halloooing filling the woods. Winter mornings when they lift off into the morning sun to feed in grain fields is a shining spectacle worthy of any national wildlife refuge.

I suspect Tom would have wished for a little more commercial forestry in the deal, just as I might have wished for something closer to a park. But here's the bottom line. A hundred years from now, depending on that future society's needs and desires, we can have either, because we were wise enough to keep the land—our ultimate option—wide open.

More than a decade after Tom died, a letter I got from Larry Walton, Tom's former boss, sums up how many of us still feel:

"There is hardly a time that I cross the Nanticoke at Sharptown and look downstream to where his office was that I don't think of Tom; or crossing the Route 50 bridge at Vienna, looking downriver to where the marshes sprawl toward his house at Henry's Crossroads and his old stomping grounds, or upstream to where we dedicated the Tom Tyler Nature Trail; or crossing the Marshy Hope at Brookview or Harrison Ferry where the Chesapeake Forest dominates the landscape…"

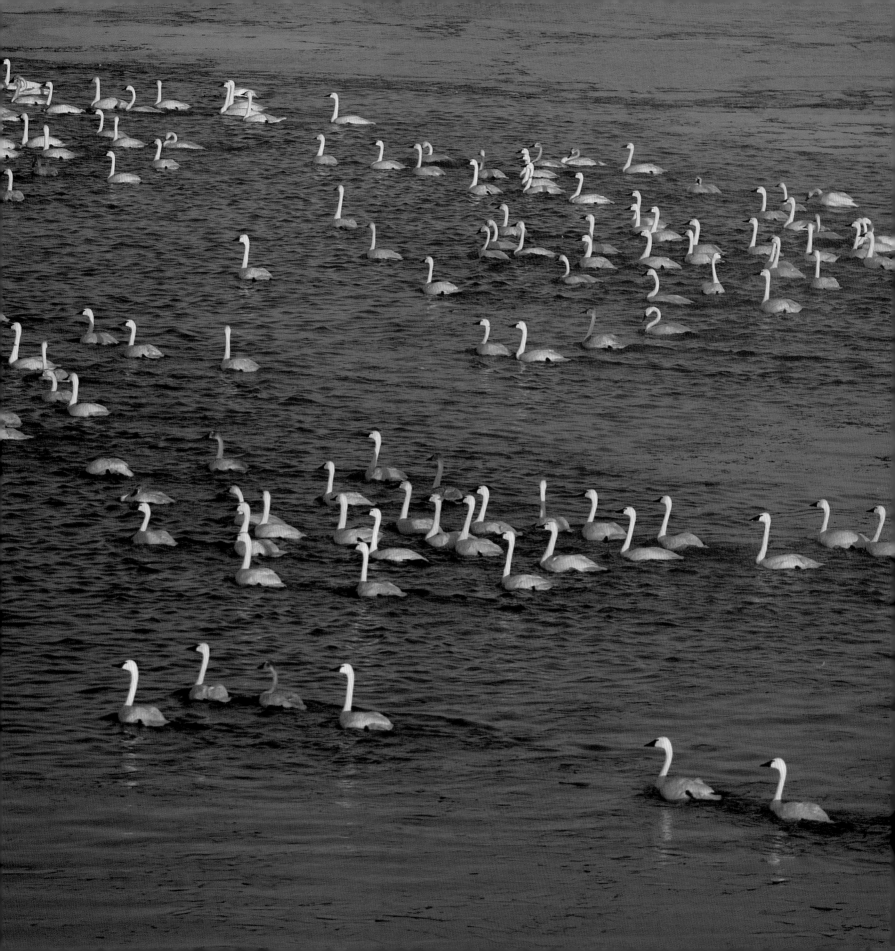

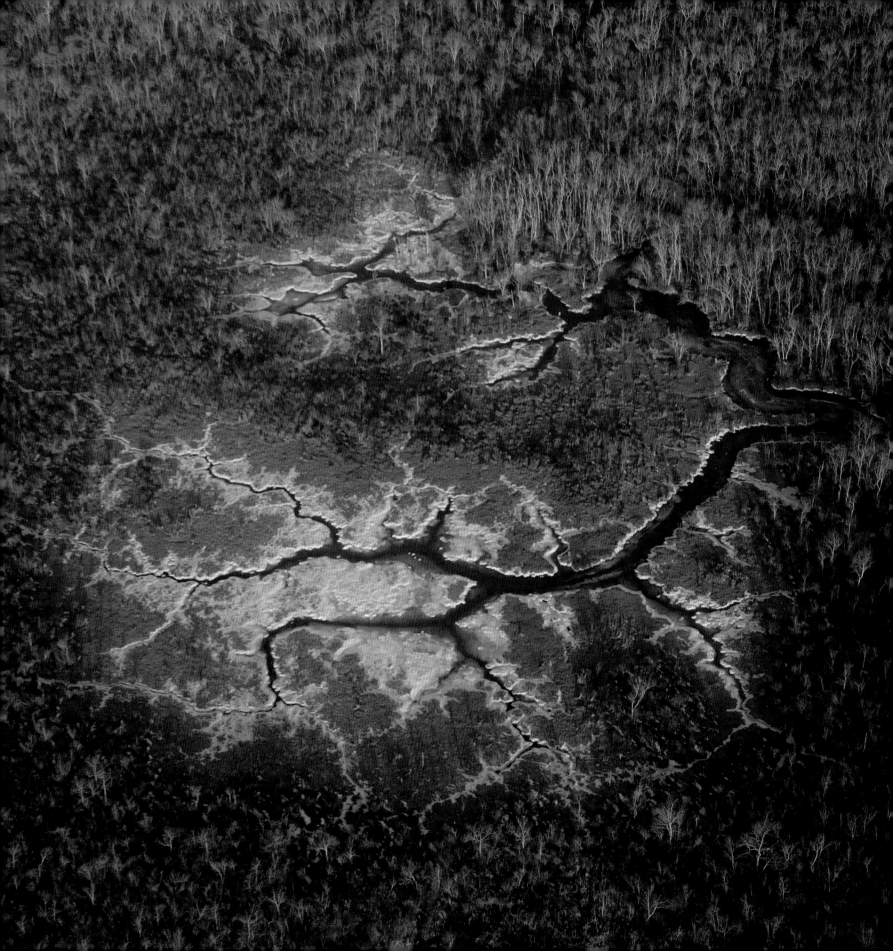

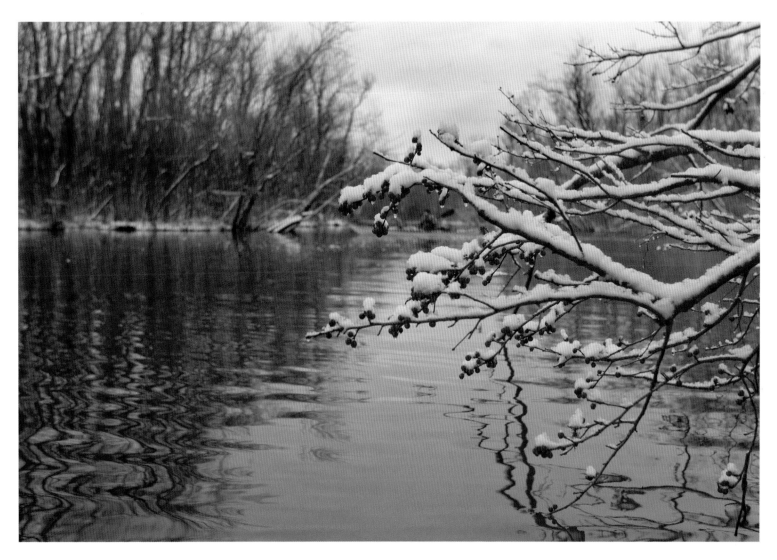

Opposite: Iced-up creeks flow in dendritic patterns among the winter forest. The same forms occur in nerve cell endings known as dendrons.

Above: Winterberry frames a kayaker on a chill December day. It is a deciduous holly, widely adapted as a yard ornamental.

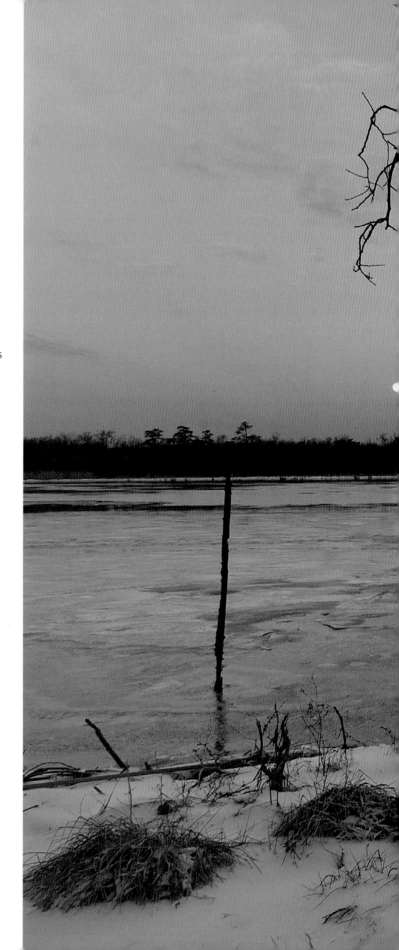

34

Moonset, ice-up, cold bones
of a fisherman's dock near
Riverton evoke February
starkly.

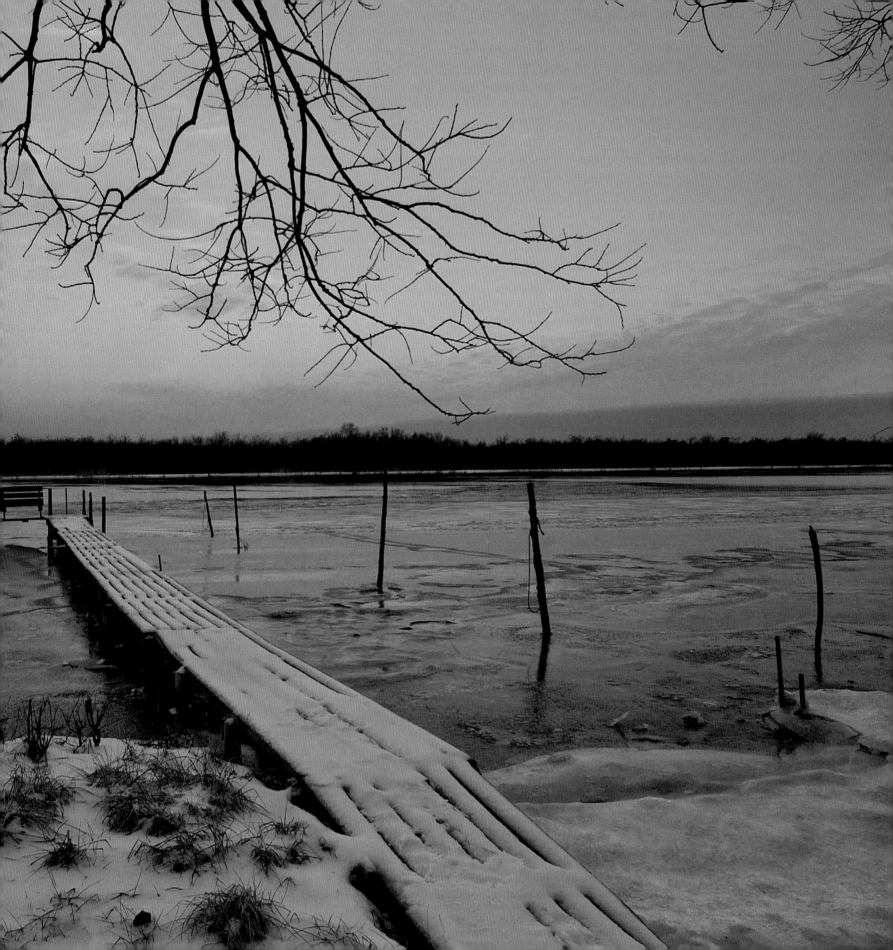

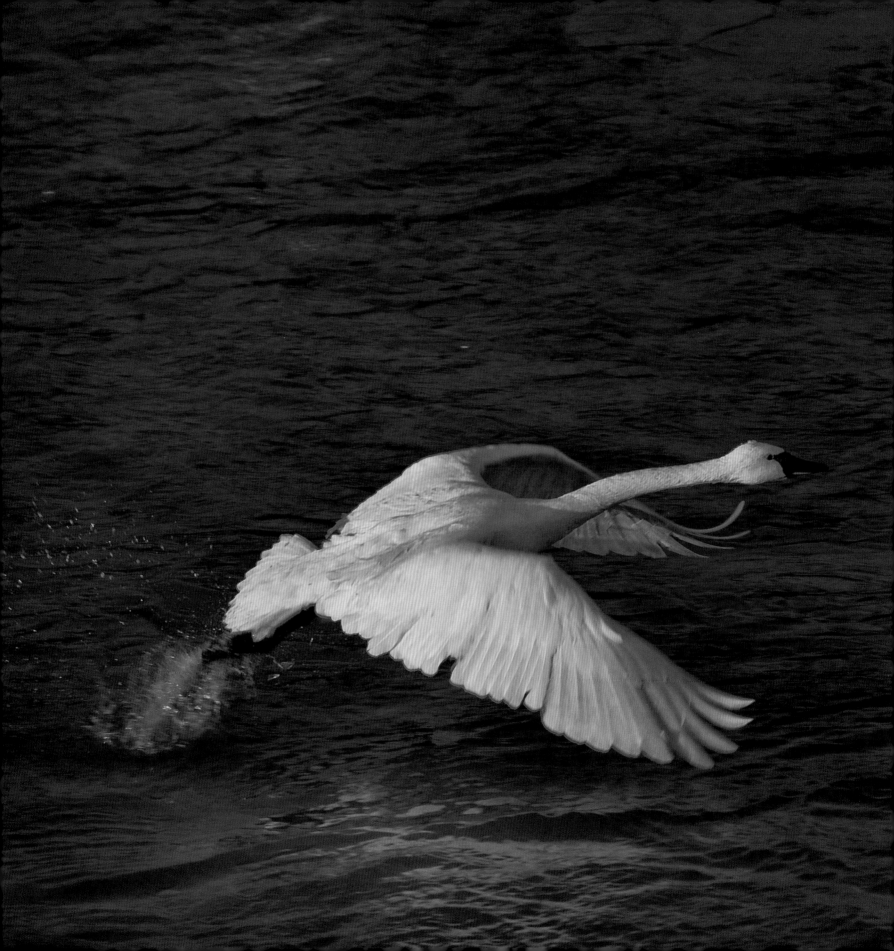

A tundra swan employs wings and big, paddle feet to achieve liftoff from the Marshy Hope. The birds roost on the river at night, feeding in surrounding corn, soybean, and wheatfields through the days. They will pull out for nesting on the Arctic tundra when March comes.

VIENNA

In the chill of a predawn April morning, the savor of roasting shad wafts across the dark river, borne on a haze of wood smoke eddying from the open cook fire glowing on Vienna's shore. The four- to seven-pound fish—split in half and affixed to long, oak planks propped alongside a hot bed of coals,—will roast for seven hours, attaining a crispy, flavorful succulence unmatchable in the best commercial kitchen. Such is the allure that the Confederate Army lost a battle in Virginia when Yankees surprised them while engrossed in a spring shad planking.

It's a scene and smell that harks back thousands of springs on this old Indian river, fabled for its great spring runs of spawning shad. Nowadays the Ruritan Club does the cooking for Vienna's popular annual Shad Festival and must go to other states for shad.

When people ask me if this quintessential Nanticoke rivertown has a future, I say that Vienna has struggled in recent decades, much like its upstream neighbors—Seaford, Federalsburg, Sharptown, Laurel—also like Bivalve, Tyaskin, and Nanticoke downstream. Everywhere commerce has moved into the big boxes and malls and industrial parks; and people's dream is to live scattered across the countryside in suburbs, exurbs, farmettes—anywhere but town.

But folks have found this place desirable for a long, long time. Vienna was laid out in its current, charming street plan more than three hundred years ago; and the area, formerly known as Emperor's Landing, was a major Indian encampment long before John Smith visited the Nanticoke four hundred years ago.

Its high, well-drained ground, strategically and gorgeously overlooking the river for miles upstream and down, made it a favored hangout now and then. The modern town is working

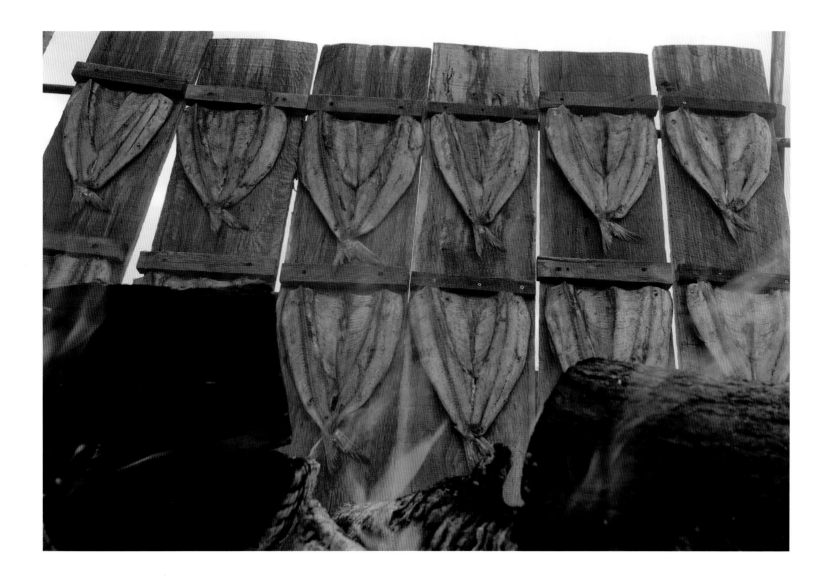

aggressively to become the site of a National Park Service visitors center along the new John Smith National Historic Water Trail; also to capitalize on ecotourism as a jumping-off point for birders, paddlers, and cyclists roaming some of the Eastern Shore's most unspoiled countryside.

Vienna is situated at a unique breakpoint in the river, about halfway between the broad, estuarine mouth around Elliott's Island and the heads of tide at Federalsburg on the Marshy Hope and Seaford on the Nanticoke.

It's where Atlantic saltwater moving up the Bay finally falls away to freshwater flowing from hundreds of thousands of acres of central Delmarva. The wetlands alongside the U.S. 50 bridge that crosses here announce the Nanticoke to millions of passersby each year: fresh green when the forests are still in winter drab; flecked with

Slabs of savory shad bake to a rich golden toothsomeness at the Vienna Shad Festival, held every April. Chesapeake rivers are all closed to taking shad, but restoration efforts are showing signs of success.

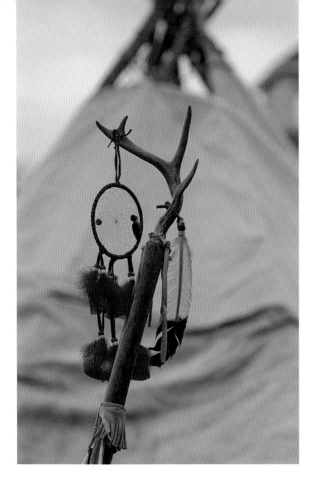

Above and right: Native Americans help celebrate the shad's return in Vienna. Shad may grow to more than seven pounds, and the roe of females is particularly prized as a spring delicacy.

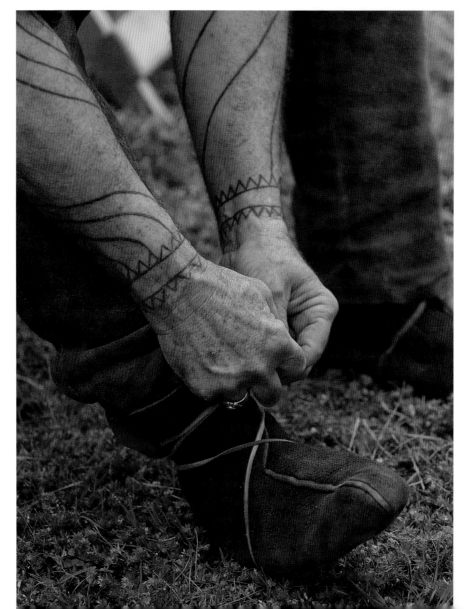

acres of creamy hibiscus blossoms in deep summer; carpeted golden with a variety of wet-footed sunflowers as autumn comes on.

Downstream from Vienna lie muskrats, black ducks and canvasbacks, blue crabs and oysters, croakers and weakfish, horseshoe crabs; and the river swinging in immense curves through vast, open saltmarsh. Upstream are beaver and otter and wood duck, largemouth bass, yellow perch; also yardlong, needle-toothed garfish; plumy wild rice and spatterdock; and the calls of owls and kingfishers reverberating along wooded corridors.

The fresh-salt interface at Vienna is where striped bass begin to spawn heaviest as they push upriver. Gathering in the Nanticoke each spring from as far away as Maine and North Carolina, "rockfish," as we call the stripers locally, can return annually for decades and attain immense size. I have seen one old Nanticoke female, an eye clouded over, that surpassed a hundred pounds, and several others from forty to sixty pounds. On April and May nights their thrashing can keep you awake, and the water in places can turn viscid with milt and roe.

The river's other aquatic bounty runs the gamut—snapping turtles, eels, catfish; also white perch, blueback and alewife herring, diamondback terrapins—even, in days long past, giant sturgeon of eight to fifteen feet. But more than any other species, *Alosa sapidissima*, the American shad, was the Nanticoke's signature fishery.

Superb on both the gourmet's fork and the sportsfisherman's line, shad have been a significant Chesapeake fishery from colonial times. George Washington depended on large hauls from the Mount Vernon shoreline for food and income. In the twentieth century, shad left ports like Crisfield by the railcarload during the peak of the spring runs. Pennsylvania historians record that Nanticoke Indians who moved north out of Maryland

and Delaware in the late 1700s continued for decades to walk back here in the spring to fish the shad runs.

The Nanticoke, for its size, was as productive of this premier species as any river of the Chesapeake. Spawning began not far above Vienna and went beyond Federalsburg, to the dam at Laurel and well above Seaford, under busy U.S. 13 to Concord Pond on Deep Creek.

The U.S. Bureau of Fisheries in 1896 ranked the Nanticoke third among Maryland shad rivers, surpassed only by the larger Choptank and Potomac. That year, more than five hundred commercial nets—from drifting gill nets to pound nets staked into the river's bed, to haul seines operated from the shorelines, took a reported 216,000 shad from the Nanticoke, about a quarter of them from Delaware. That was certainly a conservative catch estimate, given the lax requirements for reporting.

The sand and gravel nature of the Nanticoke's geology creates excellent spawning substrates along its bottom for a variety of fishes, from herring, white perch, and largemouth bass to the near extinct sturgeon—and of course the American shad. As recently as the 1960s, when I was growing up in Federalsburg, it was not uncommon to cast from the foot of the bridge in the center of town and hook half a dozen or more in an hour. At the peak of the run, I'd hide a fishing rod in the hollow of a tree behind our riverside Methodist church, in case I could slip out of Sunday school.

The good times could not last. Fishing pressure in the Nanticoke was too great. Nets often virtually cordoned off the very waters where the fish were trying to reproduce. Baywide it was the same story. Catches in Maryland, which peaked at seven million pounds in 1890, had fallen to around a million pounds annually during my

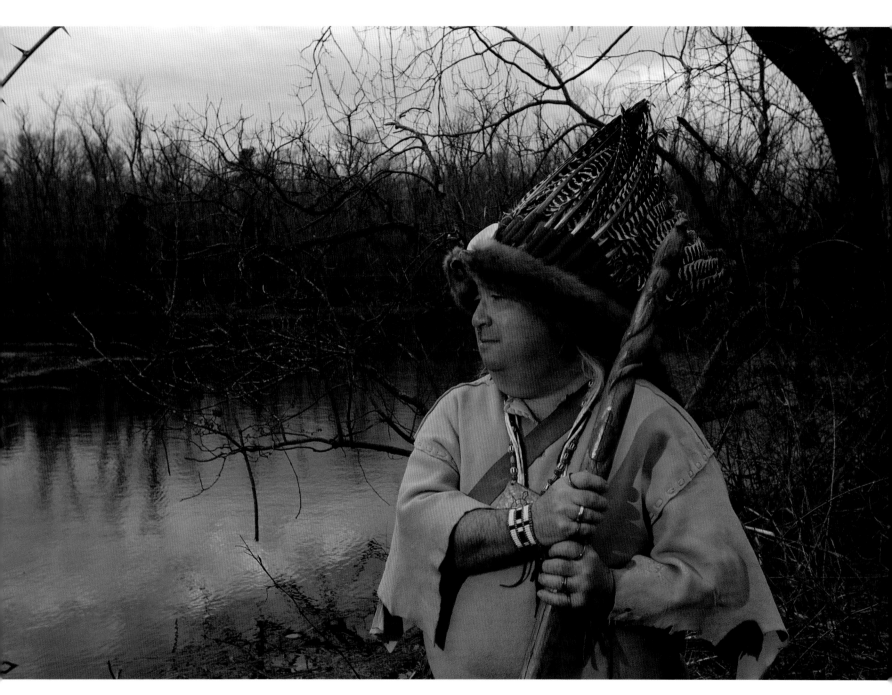

Chief Winterhawk, Sewell
Fitzhugh, leader of the
Nause Waiwash Band of
Indians, gazes over his
peoples' ancestral lands on
the banks of Chicone Creek.

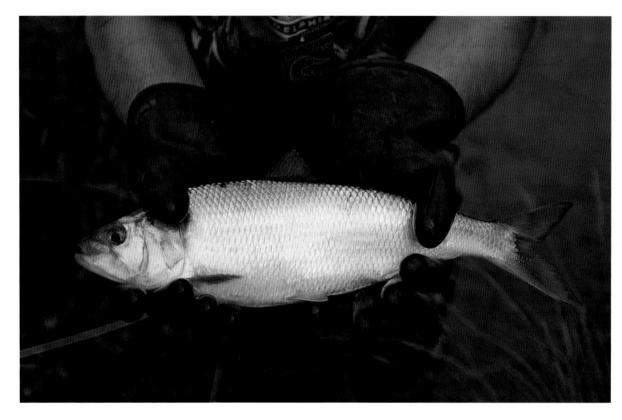

American shad, caught from just below Concord Pond in Delaware, will be used for brood stock in a hatchery run by biologist Mike Stangl and old-time fisherman Jack Knowles.

boyhood in the 1950s and '60s. That was once roughly the catch in the Nanticoke alone.

By the 1970s shad catches were in freefall. Statewide reported catches plummeted to half a million pounds in 1973, then a hundred thousand pounds in 1976—then just over twenty thousand pounds in 1979. There was scarcely a fisherman left to whimper when Maryland, under threat of a lawsuit by sportsfishermen, closed its shad season for the first time in history in 1980.

Despite a closed season for twenty-seven years now, the species has not been able to come back on most rivers, including the Nanticoke. A few fishermen who persisted in the Delaware por-

tion of the river landed a total of seventy-three pounds of shad when that state finally closed the season in 1999.

The Nanticoke lost more than fish. It lost a unique portion of its culture: the springtime rituals of readying boats and gear in all the little river towns; the anticipation on calm April mornings as lines of corks curved artfully across the water's surface, buoying nets drifting below on the tide, diving under as schools of fish struck and weighed them down.

Virtually gone, too, are the slender, graceful little "shad barges," twenty-two- to twenty-four-foot flatbottom skiffs. Single, broad planks of

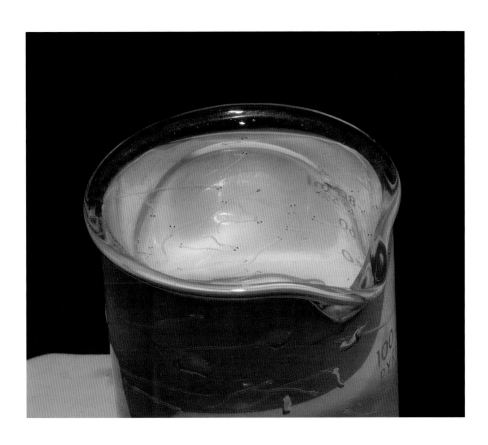

Newly hatched shad wriggle in a beaker at Mike Stangl's riverside hatchery just above Broad Creek.

cedar or pine were bent to make their sides. Their gunwales sloped low to the water to facilitate hauling in the catch. They were designed explicitly for netting shad: "wan't nothing else that would give satisfaction . . . a ton of shad wouldn't tell one of them boats nothin'," the late Powell Horseman, an old barge builder, said.

And I, who first connected with the Chesapeake and the oceans by hooking shad for sport far upstream in Federalsburg, have raised two kids to adulthood who never cast a line for them. My concern here is not selfish. Across the Chesapeake, no one who has moved here or been born since the 1970s has known the great estuary when its major ecosystems and fisheries were more intact. At some point soon, "save the shad" and "save the Bay" might fall on uncomprehending ears.

But, just maybe, the shad situation is starting to look up. On a late April morning, as blossoming dogwood festoons the riverbanks, Mike Stangl, a Delaware state biologist, stands stirring fertilized shad eggs with a turkey quill in big glass jars. This will help them hatch all at the same time, he explains. As sunlight streams through the jars, you can see the wriggling embryos about to pop forth.

Stangl works from a plain, twenty-by-forty-foot building tucked into the woods just a few miles downstream from Seaford. Nearby, obscured by vegetation, is an old netters' shack, where commercial shad fishermen passed the time while their nets drifted through a long "rech" (a reach, or straight) between bends of the river.

Nanticoke water pumps through a fifteen-foot diameter tank that holds some fifty swirling male and female shad, all close to releasing their roe and milt. Round tanks are critical. Shad are skittish and fragile fish and will swim themselves to death if they get in a corner, the biologist says. From his modest hatchery, Stangl has already hatched and released a hundred thousand three-day-old fry. He's shooting for close to half a million this year, up from 260,000 last year.

He's using native spawning stock, caught below the dam at Concord Pond on Deep Creek. Imprinting should be good, he says, ensuring that survivors return, salmon-like, to their birth river after three to five years in the ocean. The fry before release spend a few hours in a chemical bath that will distinctly mark their inner ear bones when viewed under a special light. That way scientists can tell whether returning adults are a result of the hatchery.

Stangl's operation is a drop in the bucket compared to the million upon million of fry from natural spawning in healthier days for the shad. It'll be 2010 or later before he sees any appreciable returns from the sea.

But he's ramping up production each year. And Maryland is beginning to stock little shad on the Marshy Hope. In the Choptank, Patuxent, Potomac, James, Susquehanna, and other Bay rivers, such stocking is farther along and is working. Returns of wild fish are gradually outstripping returns of hatchery-born shad, the key to a self-sustaining population.

Stangl goes out on the river with an electro-shock device to stun and bring to the surface

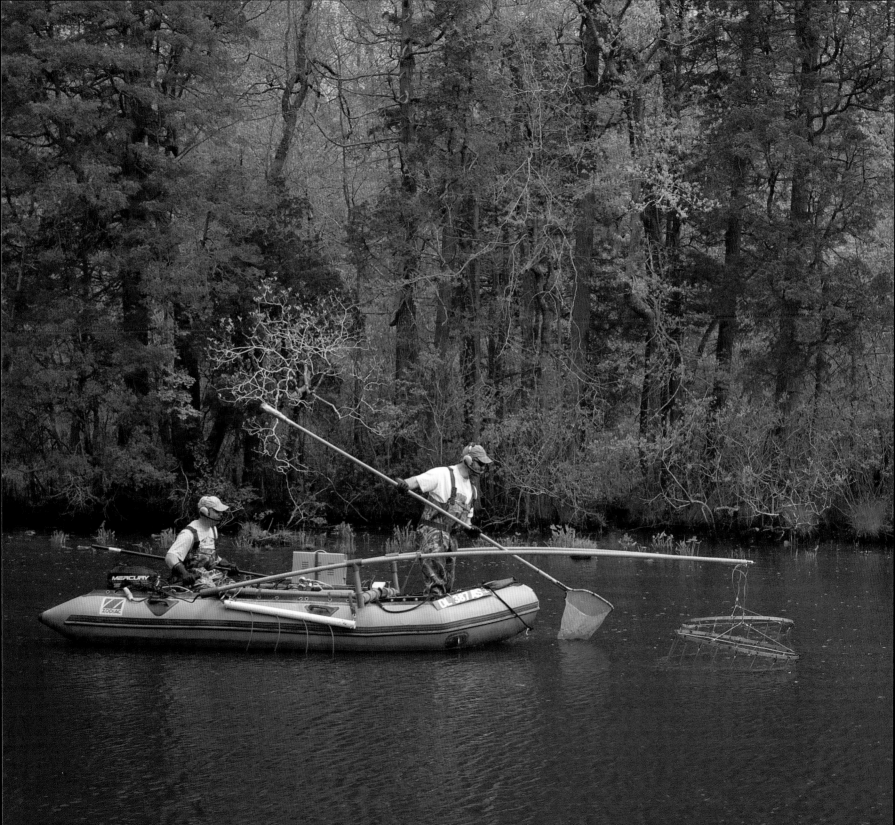

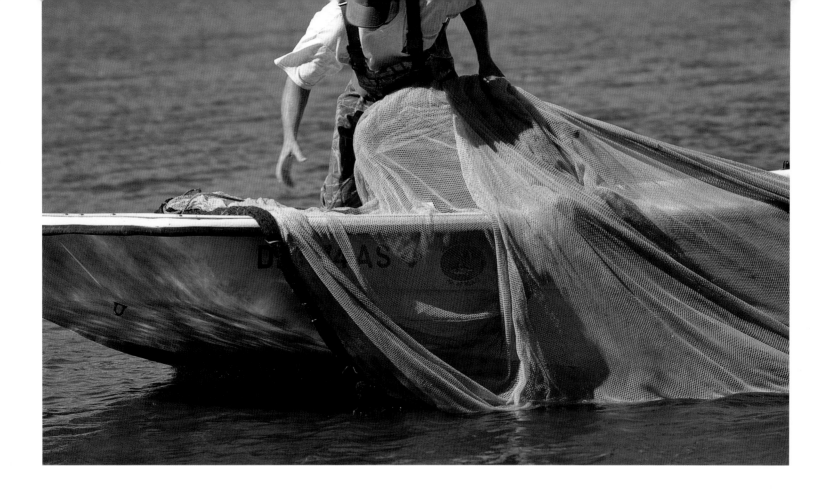

three- to four-pound spawning shad for his
spawning tanks. "Bass fishermen see them coming
up and their jaws just drop," he says; "they had no
idea fish like that were even here."

Stangl's assistant is 64-year-old Jack Knowles,
whose ancestors settled on a bend of the Nanticoke just below Woodland Ferry in Delaware
in the 1700s. He's one of the last of the river's
commercial shad netters, taught to fish when he
was five by his grandfather and grandmother.
He grew up hearing old fishermen talk of horses
and buggies lined up by the Nanticoke's shores
to buy herring to salt away in casks and crocks.
A smaller relative of the shad, herring once

thronged every free-flowing little creek on the
upper Nanticoke to spawn, thick enough that
one could dip them up with a hand net. They
are coming back too, now that fishing pressure is
reduced.

"I'll never be allowed to net shad commercially
again, but that's all right, I've had my time,"
Knowles says.

But the time when we can once again angle for
shad—there is no better light tackle fun on tidal
rivers of the Bay—could return within the next
decade or so. That would end a nearly forty-year
drought on the Nanticoke, two generations of
kids born and grown without some of the best

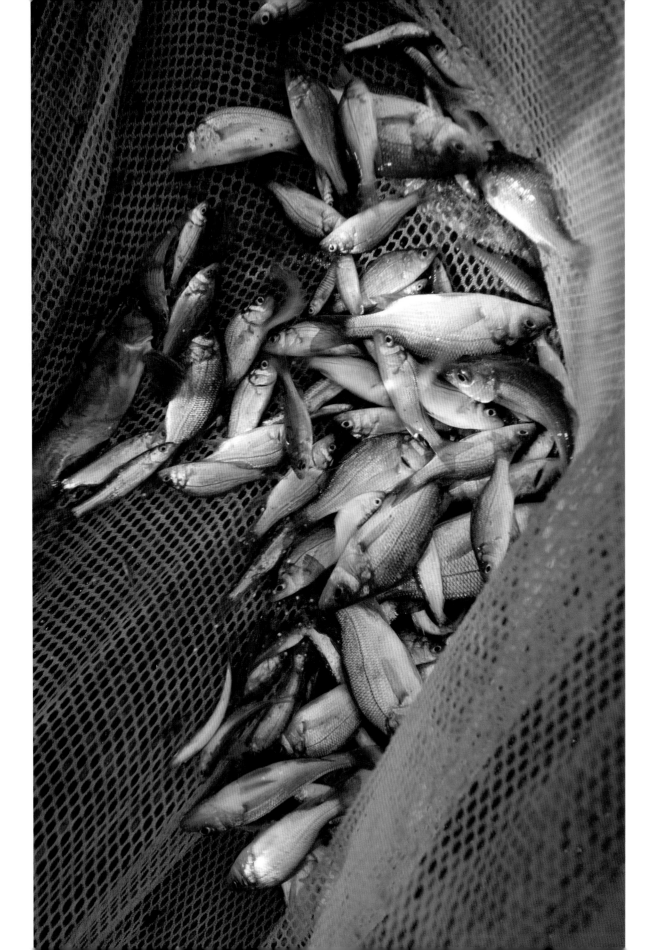

the river had to offer. It could also draw fishing dollars into the struggling river towns.

Now it's late summer. Goldenrod is flowering along the river's banks, cardinal flower blossoms bright red from the swamp edges, and redtwig dogwood is in full berry. Three ospreys overhead are taking turns harassing a bald eagle. I've driven up to Federalsburg to join Brian Richardson and a crew of Maryland biologists who are seining the edges of the Marshy Hope to sample for juvenile shad, the fruit of any spawning that occurred successfully the previous spring. Over in Delaware, Stangl will be doing the same thing.

Both are finding some, but not many, about what they expect at this point. Both teams also note that it gets harder every year to find places on the shore from which to seine. Development, stone riprap, bulkheads, all signs of human "progress" are hardening more and more of the river shores everywhere up and down the Bay.

On the way into Federalsburg I pass a big blue-and-white striped tent with a sign: Old Time Revival with Chief Apostle John C. McCollum. At the time I thought little of it.

Then, at our first seine station by the bridge where I hooked my first shad fifty springs ago (or did it hook me?), we leap from the bow of the biologists' skiff into the river, splashing thigh deep to deploy the seine. And a town cop races toward us in his cruiser. "Are you with the revival?" he wants to know.

I realize later he thought an unauthorized baptism was in progress. And I guess we were looking for salvation of a sort—the April morning when my kids could come here and hook into something silver and exciting; when downriver in Vienna, people can eat shad from their own river again.

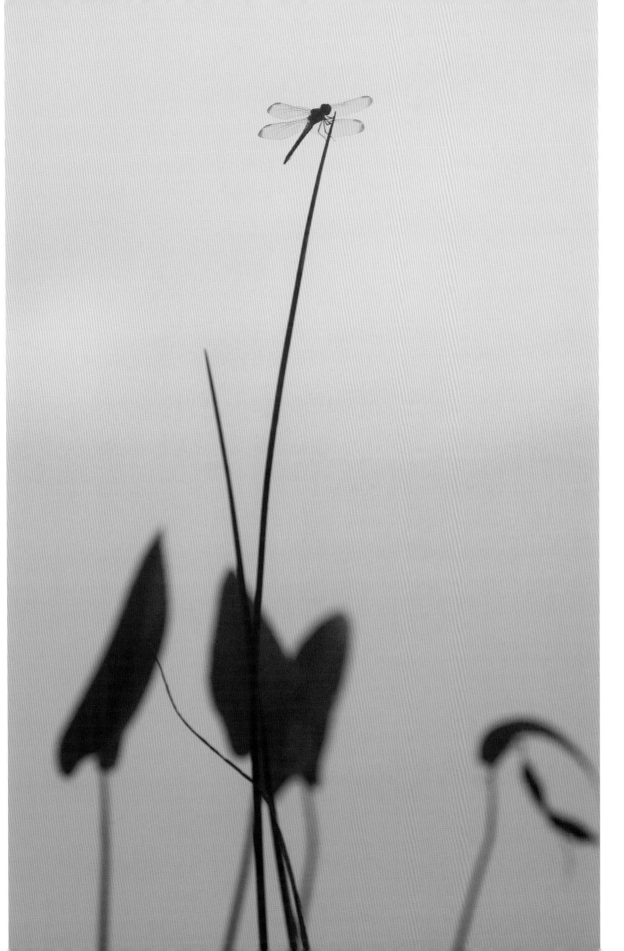

Left: Golden evening light burnishes the wings of a dragonfly perching atop a scirpus, a slender reed beloved by muskrats for food.

Overleaf: Wild rice, *Zazinia aquatica*, waves in the late August breeze at the mouth of Broad Creek as an osprey patrols.

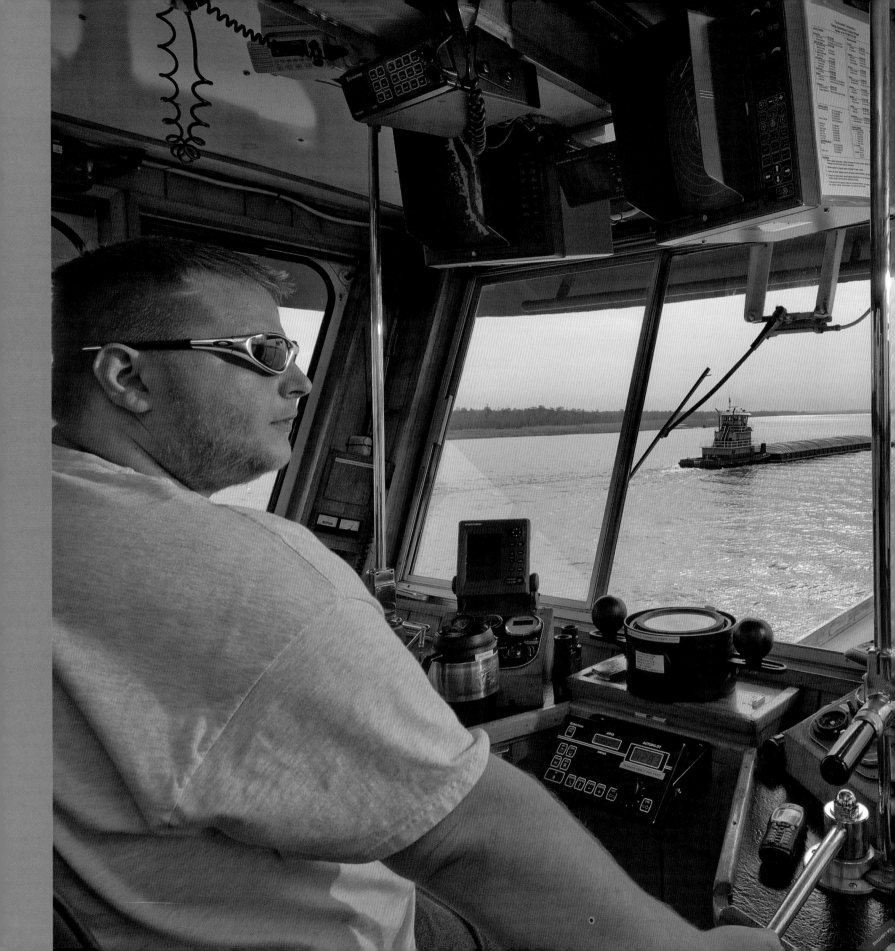

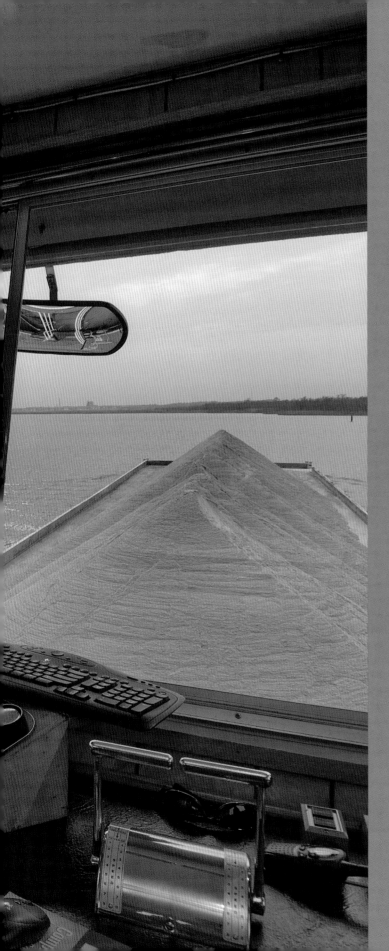

Tuggers

I'm basking in afternoon sun, propped against a twenty-foot sand dune, watching the river slide by, silent except for a gentle breeze, the mewing of gulls and the swish of wavelets.

Right behind me is a hundred yards of steel barge and tugboat, more than a thousand horsepower churning twin, five-foot diameter props, moving ten million pounds smoothly down the Nanticoke. My "dune" on the barge's broad bow, and another eighteen piles of mined sand bound for Baltimore, blots out all sight and sound of the roaring tug, pushing from behind.

The Nanticoke is the most commercial of all Eastern Shore rivers, plied by seagoing barges most days of the year, sometimes several a day. Lit up at night, their passage is a marvelous juxtaposition along the narrow corridors of forest and marsh.

No dredging is required to maintain channel depths of fifteen to thirty feet along much of the forty-odd mile run from the river's mouth to Seaford, Delaware. The controlling, or least, depth is around nine feet, about what a loaded, 250-foot barge draws. A few deep holes are close to fifty feet.

My perch out in front of the tug, *Night Falcon*, may be the best way to see the Nanticoke. May be—Jimmy Hess,

Opposite: Jimmy Hess pushes a load of sand downriver on the *Night Falcon*. A grain tug has just passed him to port.

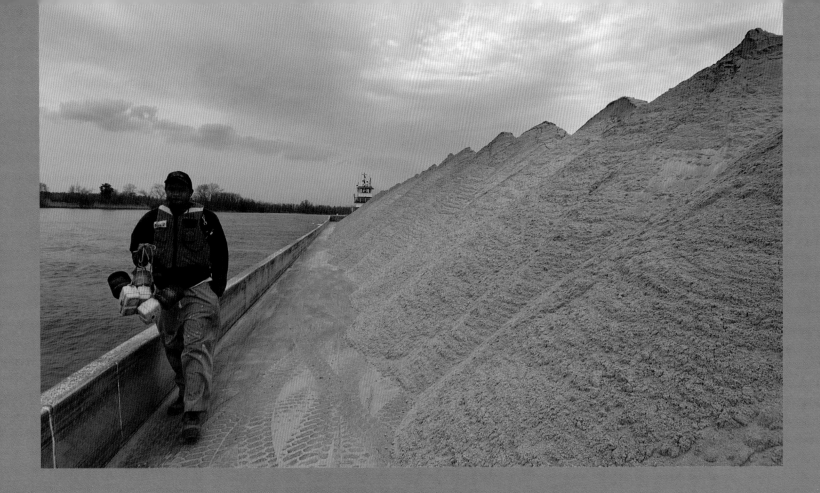

Ricky Styles strides to the bow to place night running lights as evening gathers.

who's driving us downriver this fine spring afternoon, doesn't have a shabby view either. He looks out from the tug's comfortably furnished, climate-controlled pilot house, three stories up, encased by broad, smoked glass windows on three sides. Up here the roaring diesels are a whisper. We converse easily in normal voices.

"Can't beat it…you see a lot of sunsets and sunrises from here, see wild turkeys feeding out in the marsh, see bald eagles, swans, all the waterfowl, honk at kids playing on the shoreline," Hess says.

But hour after hour, his attention never wavers from the task at hand. He makes constant, subtle course corrections, alternately pushing and pulling on chrome steering levers to either side of his seat. He constantly glances at an array of depth sounders and a GPS that tracks the tug relative to the river's channel.

Though deep for a Bay river, the Nanticoke's channel is not a lot wider than the tug and barge in places. There's no room for error in some of the bends—and the big U.S. 50 bridge at Vienna slants sharply across the channel, requiring captains to thread a needle with their 250-foot barges. The battered sheet steel and gouged timbers buffering the bridge's supports are proof that not every tug makes it through unscathed.

At the confluence of the Marshy Hope Creek and main Nanticoke where a sharp left turn is required, the lone channel marker is of minimal help. Hess lines up a tall loblolly pine against a notch in the hardwood forest to navigate through.

The work, Hess says, is fourteen days on, fourteen off, and by the end of such a shift he's missing his wife and little daughter back in Virginia. The concept of docking in different ports may seem romantic, or at

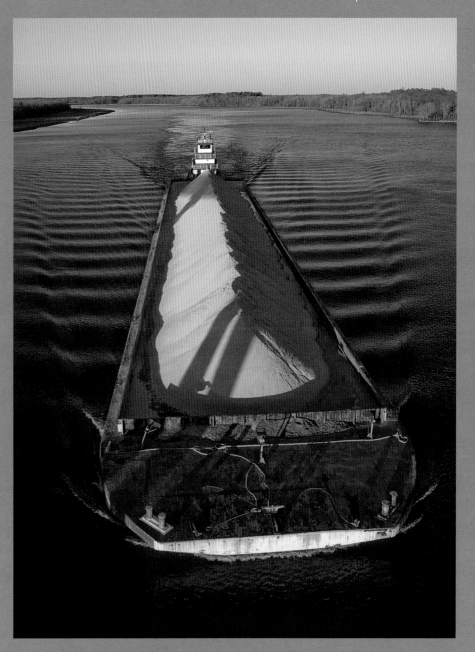

least interesting, but it's pretty much fiction. The *Night Falcon* barely stops running unless repairs are needed. When it brings a barge of Western Shore rock into Seaford, a barge of Eastern Shore sand is already loaded and waiting to be hitched up—turnaround time is less than half an hour.

Hess will motor today from noon until six, from Seaford to the river's mouth. The *Night Falcon*'s captain, Pete Luikert, will take over, and Hess will eat in the tug's well-stocked little kitchen, go to his blacked-out room and watch movies and catch three hours' sleep before he's on again at midnight. At the end of his next shift he'll get a good night's sleep.

By then the tug will have dropped its sand at Brooklyn in the Patapsco River's Middle Branch and headed for the Susquehanna at Bay's head to pick up another load of rock. Then it's back to Seaford, or perhaps up the Potomac to where they are building the new Washington Nationals baseball stadium.

Other barge companies haul grain and heating oil up and down the river. In 2002, a certificate on the cabin wall shows, the *Night Falcon* hauled a record 637,437 tons of sand, gravel, and rock. A captain, Hess says, can make upward of $60,000 a year with his company, Salisbury Towing, which operates seven tugs.

"I like this job...you show up wearing what you want to wear, shave or don't shave, your choice. You get one phone call a day from your boss who tells you where to go next and you go. It's not like a factory."

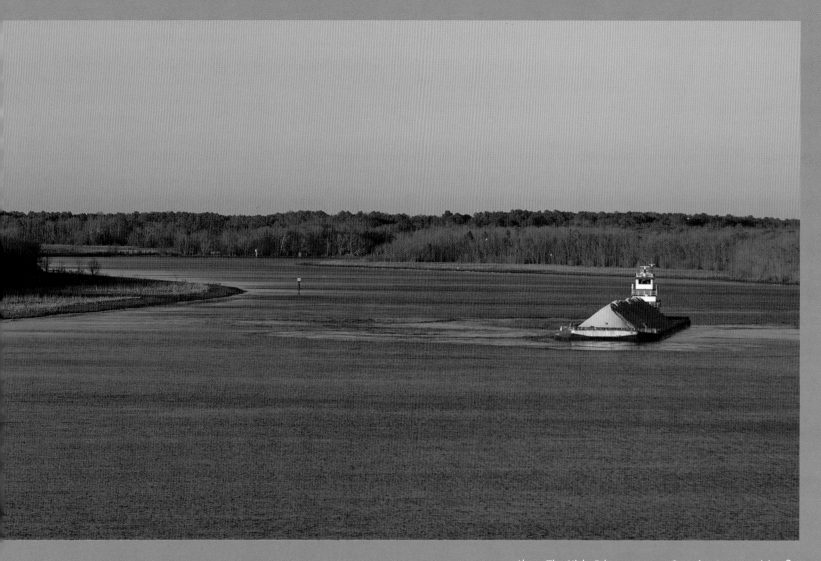

Above: The *Night Falcon* rounds a bend and sets course for the center span of the Route 213 bridge at Sharptown.

Opposite: A competitive fleet out of Cedar Hill Marina races every Thursday night in the summer, braving thunderstorms and calms that both occur frequently on the broad lower Nanticoke.

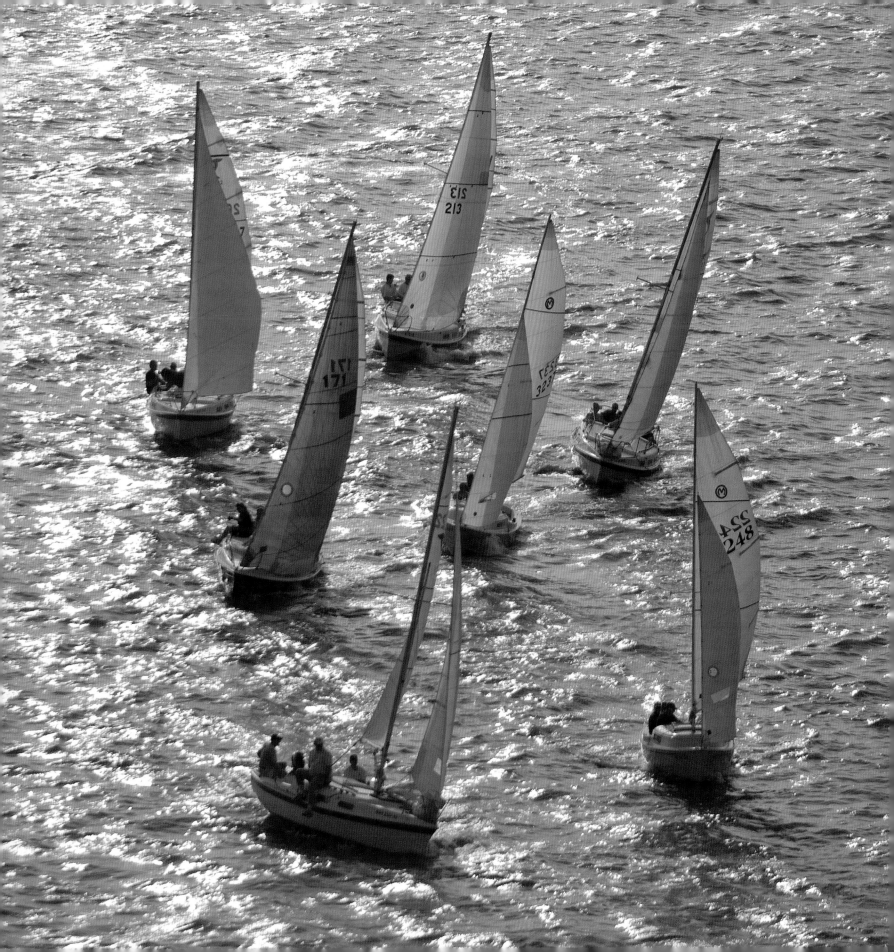

The first moonset of the
year reflects wanly as a pink
sunrise colors the river off
the photographer's front
yard.

LOWER RIVER

Frost coats our skiff. A round November moon is setting to the west over Elliott's Island. It gleams through the diamond meshes of the pound, an elaborate maze of thick-corded net rising above our heads and staked across maybe half an acre in midriver, half a mile from either shore. The sturdy poles that hold it in place sway and gurgle in the pull of big ebb currents flexing under the river's smooth skin. Expectant great blue herons perch in the net's rigging. A calling loon quavers up the dawn.

On clear days like this, you can see across maybe a hundred square miles of untrammeled marsh where the Nanticoke and adjacent Fishing Bay and Blackwater River drainages merge into Tangier Sound. Here is a third of all Maryland's tidal wetlands—"the Chesapeake's Everglades," naturalist Paul Spitzer has called them. It is some of North America's most important waterfowl habitat. It is a watery wilderness through which we annually paddle for four days, encountering only three rural roads in some sixty miles.

You almost expect to see smoke rising from the long-gone Indian village of Nause, which John Smith charted here when he entered the Nanticoke four centuries ago. Whump! Whump! Whump! A duck hunter's 12-gauge from the distant marsh breaks the spell.

Two beamy, mud-streaked skiffs appear on the horizon, closing fast. The Calloways have beaten us out, already checked their nets down at the river's mouth. With a friendly nod, but all business, the two brothers and their two grown sons set silently to work, untying one side of the pound, a squarish enclosure where fish become trapped after entering the "throat," an underwater mesh funnel. A fence of net extends from the pound for a hundred yards or more from the throat to intercept fish moving along the river and shepherd them into the trap.

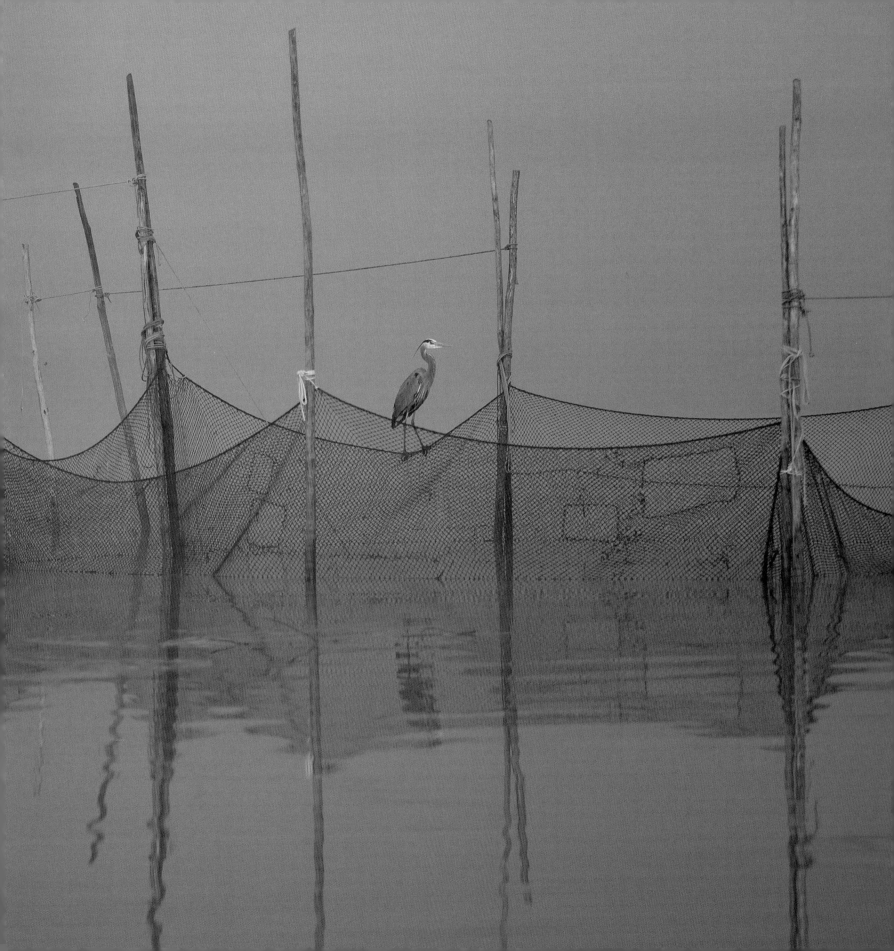

The pound easily accommodates their twenty-four-foot skiff. It begins to boil as the men tighten the net, hauling it in hand over hand, bringing up a thrashing, squirming mass of flounder, rockfish, crabs, white perch, and gizzard shad. The men scoop up the fish with a sturdy dip net and sort them by size and species into plastic milk crates, discarding undersize or nonmarket species.

No matter how many times you do this, the netters say, there is always anticipation as the catch comes to the surface. The massive head of a black drum, maybe seventy pounds, heaves above the fray; also a two-foot sturgeon, a baby that could reach fifteen feet and eight hundred pounds half a century from now. In 1996 Maryland biologists stocked 3,700 little sturgeon in the Nanticoke. These have moved out to sea, and any surviving females won't return to spawn until around 2010, when they will be around seven feet long.

If anything could be mistaken as the legendary sea monster, Chessie, it would be a big sturgeon. The prehistoric-looking bottom feeders, prized for both meat and caviar, have remained scarce in Bay rivers since the 1950s, when fishing for them was closed. The Calloways tell the story of their grandfather, Will. To snare sturgeon he drifted gill nets of gigantic size, fifteen-inch meshes, measured corner to corner. He had three healthy specimens tied to the dock at long-gone Athaloo Landing, keeping them fresh for the steamer that would take them to urban markets; but the fish slipped the hitches he had fastened around their deeply forked tails.

No one counts on a sturgeon comeback. It's uncertain whether any spawning females are left and whether the degraded Chesapeake still has enough of the cool, oxygen-rich waters they

Opposite: Looking for lunch, a great blue heron sentinels a pound net south of Vienna.

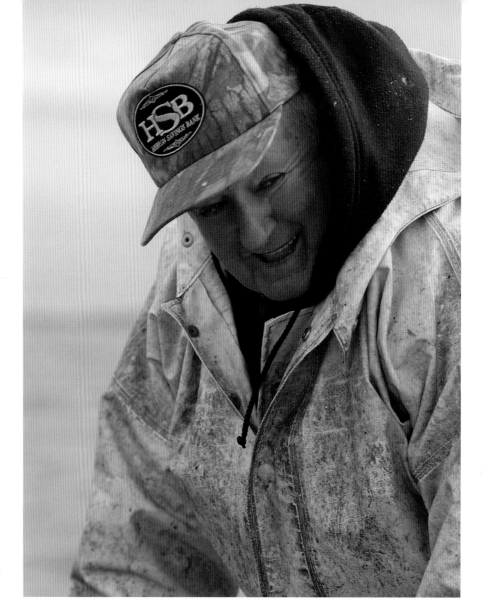

Billy Calloway, dressed for cool spring mornings, tends his nets.

prefer. Small ones like those the Calloways catch could be wanderers from the Hudson or Delaware river systems. But reports of immature sturgeon caught by Bay fishermen reached a record 450 in 2006, and a 170-pound female with eggs was caught a few rivers north of the Nanticoke in 2007. "I would not be shocked to find spawning in the Nanticoke," a federal biologist told me.

As the Calloways head upriver to fish more nets a lone oyster tonger heads out of the little watermen's harbor to our south in the village of Nanticoke. It's most likely Harry and Paula Insley in the forty-two-foot workboat *Lisa Mae II*. The couple have made their living from the lower Nanticoke for forty years, trotlining blue crabs in summers, hand tonging oysters in fall and winter. Harry drives and catches, Paula culls and sorts the oysters and crabs.

White perch, snared on
their March spawning run,
are bound for market in
Cambridge.

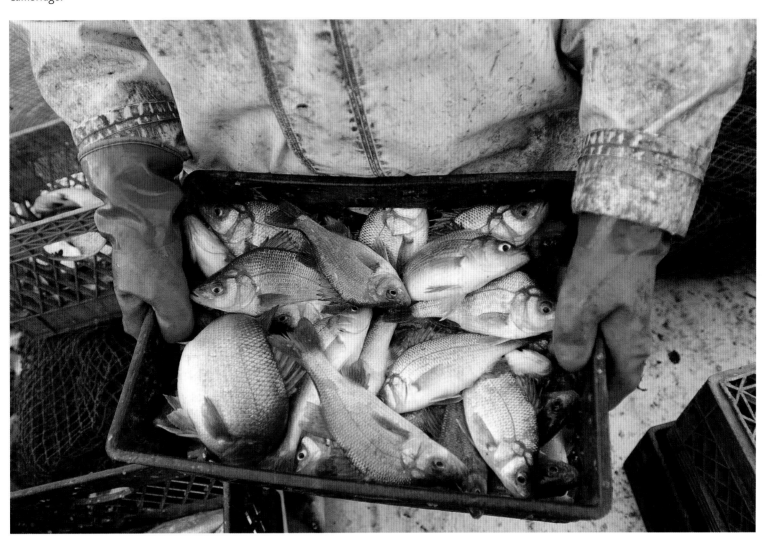

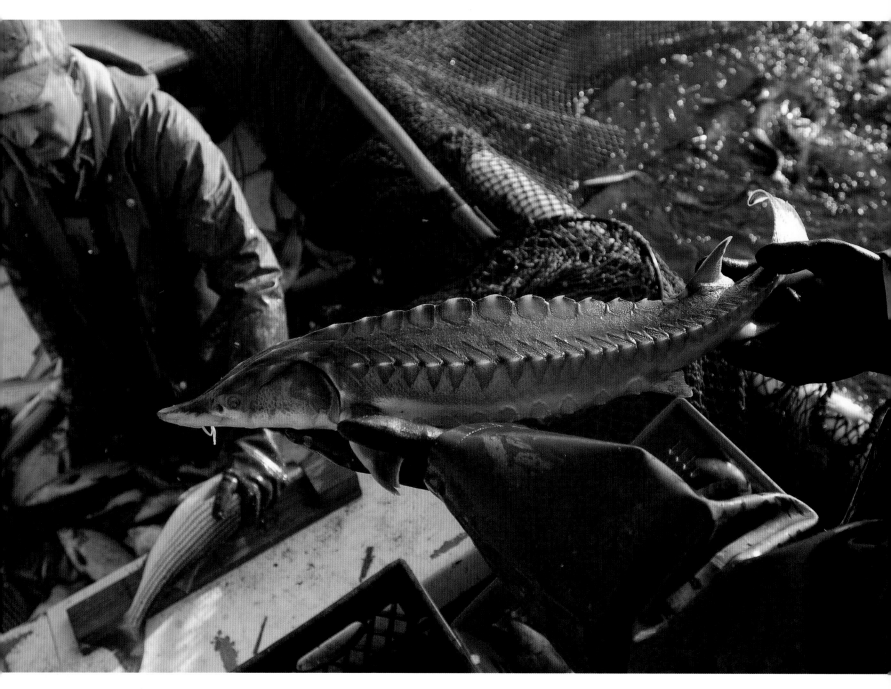

Netting in November, a small sturgeon will be returned to the river, to grow perhaps to twelve feet several decades from now. Female sturgeon do not reach sexual maturity until they are about seven feet long. To date there is no evidence that the once-abundant sturgeon have resumed spawning in the Nanticoke.

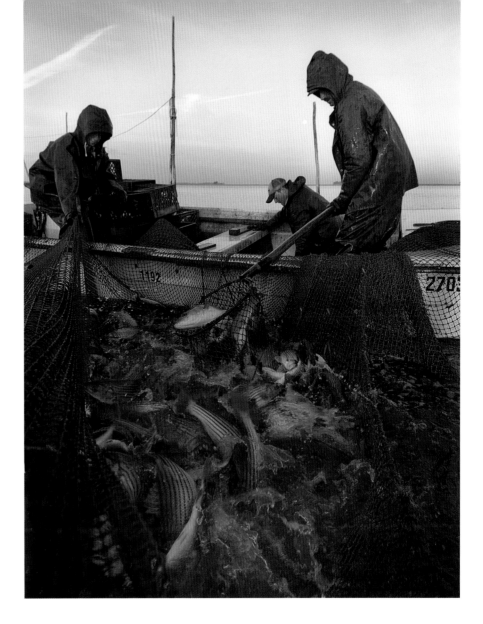

They've watched crabbing boats in the Nanticoke go from dozens to a dozen in recent summers. A respectable little fleet of oystermen used to sally forth from Nanticoke Harbor, but nowadays two other boats would seem like a crowd, they say.

In Bivalve, another lower Nanticoke community, Wilbur Messick used to make and sell two hundred pairs of fine-grained, heart pine oyster tong shafts a year. Now it's maybe seventy pairs in a good year, with most sales going to Virginia and to Delaware Bay tongers. His workshop is where the Messick family in prior generations made pine caskets and embalmed bodies in their funeral business. It was a natural extension, he says, to make oyster tongs.

Paula Insley says retirement is not in her and Harry's plans. The river will continue to be their full-time living. "But the older watermen are gone, and it doesn't seem like the young ones are doing much." Their four grown kids all work on land.

"Few men of the sort who leave legends appear to have settled on its banks," says Hulbert Footner's chapter on the Nanticoke in *Rivers of the Eastern Shore*. Indeed, the official list's a short one: John Henry, a Maryland governor and U.S. senator whose estate, Weston, stands just

Striped bass fill the Calloways' nets off Sandy Hill. The species' comeback is a major Chesapeake success story.

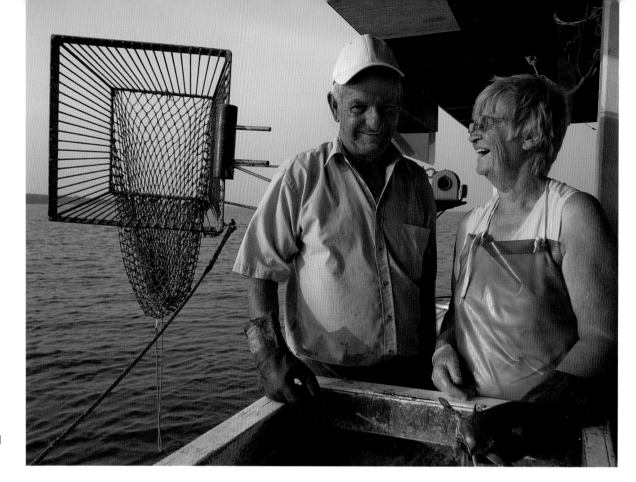

Harry and Paula Insley trotline for blue crabs off the town of Nanticoke in summertime. They've spent three decades aboard together.

upstream of the Calloways' pound net; the famous Lee family of Virginia who settled in Rehoboth on the Marshy Hope in the 1670s; Patty Cannon, a bloody sort who lived around Broad Creek—she confessed in 1829 to eleven murders, including her husband and baby.

But this says more about how we write history, focused on wars and wealth, on politics and crime. As counterpoint, consider the Calloways, who invest themselves in and are evocative of the Nanticoke region to a degree we should celebrate more.

From their Hungry Neck Farm in western Wicomico County, they till more than 3,500

acres and raise close to a million chickens. From fall until spring, when many farmers take a well-deserved break, the Calloways fish as many as twenty-five commercial nets along fifteen miles of Nanticoke River and creeks.

In their spare time they trap for fur and meat in the river's marshes, taking up to five thousand muskrats; also drift gill nets for rockfish and white perch; grow and market direct to city buyers enough vegetables and melons to keep a camping trailer, manned by family members, in New Jersey all summer.

At one time or another they have tried about everything the region has to offer: oystering, eel

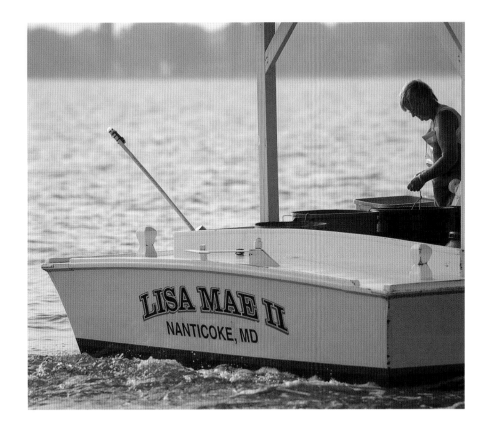

Paula Insley sorts crabs aboard the Lisa Mae II in July...

potting, raising hogs and cattle, making sausage and scrapple; "turkling" (catching snapping turtles), trapping coons and foxes, hunting deer, making and selling Christmas wreaths of the glossy, dark green crowsfoot they pick from their woods.

The family, brothers Billy and Eddie and their two sons, Tommy and David, have become keepers of otherwise-lost knowledge of the once-great Nanticoke fisheries—how to use the pound net. A pound net is a seriously complex affair, involving more than one hundred poles, each the size of a small tree, pounded by hand four to six feet into the river's bed. Attached to these is a complicated series of overlapping mesh panels, tensioned by myriad ropes, that guide fish through an underwater mesh funnel, or "throat" into a terminal enclosure, or pound.

To catch well, such a net must be located and set up precisely, virtually fine-tuned to each part of the river. The Calloways design and build from scratch all the nets they use. Tommy, the family's true netmeister, keeps cards on which he records the spacing of poles and layout of each net as it is taken up each season. He discourses easily on the intricacies of proper throat design, as well as the "wings" and the "backing," the "hedging," the "nose," the "lacing in," and other

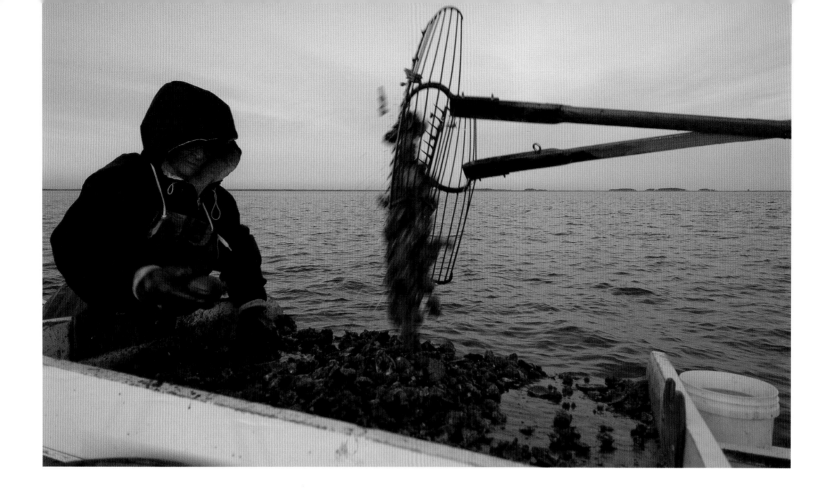

…and a few months later she culls oysters as her husband tongs them aboard.

terms more the province of old-time watermen than farmers. "A bought net simply will not catch with ours," he explains.

Deployed separately or sometimes attached to the larger pound nets are fykes—long, mesh bags, held open by a series of hoops. Fish pass farther and farther into the fyke through a series of interior nets that narrow to a throat. Fykes work better, for example, on white perch, which won't "trail," or follow the long fence into the pound like rockfish will.

The family makes money off of fishing, but it's a minor part of the combined incomes of their families (Some of the wives have office jobs, one

drives a school bus, and all help with farm work). They would hate to figure what they make per hour from fish, the men say.

At the heart of the matter, one suspects, is that they just love to fish. And probably the river plays a role—if you had to pick a place in Maryland or Delaware that would allow a family like the Calloways to exist, it would be here.

From below Vienna, the Nanticoke sashays for miles in a series of great bends and straights. Throughout this distance, along the Wicomico shore, each curve of the river embraces vast marshes, run through by hundreds of miles of cricks, guts, sloughs, dreens, ditches, canals, inlets, thoroughfares, and assorted other drainage-ways. Jutting riverward behind these wetlands are a series of farmed and forested "necks"—Athel, Hurley, Nutters, Wetipquin, and others. All have ready access to the main river through four major creeks—Barren, Rewastico, Quantico, and Wetipquin—that run for miles into the county's interior.

Seen from a satellite, this is unique in the whole six-state, 64,000-square-mile watershed of the Chesapeake. There simply is no other arrangement like these undeveloped reaches of the Nanticoke, where fish and fowl, cropland, marshland, and tidal waterways conspire so sympathetically. It is a place to be farmed and fished, hunted and trapped, plowed and timbered and netted; a place that yields nearly everything water and soil on Maryland's lower Eastern Shore can aspire to.

The Calloways can recall when every reach of the river—the straights between bends where nets can be drifted on the tides—had its own name and stories of big catches and events: the Stumps, Chicone, Tide Mill, Steam Mill, Peach Orchard, Shallow Ground. They have incorporated the techniques and net designs of the river's old-time fishermen into their own fishing.

You wonder whether it can continue this way. The family has a small crop of successors coming up. Two grandsons and a nephew are beginning to learn the nets. Ultimately it will depend on the Nanticoke—but more than that on the river's watershed. The links are strong and clear between what we do on the land and the quality and liveliness of our waters. The Chesapeake and its tidal rivers reflect our behavior, for good or ill. In recent decades the picture in the mirror hasn't been pretty.

OPTIONS

We've taken a grand old ramble down the "pristine" Nanticoke, from a boater's view, a fisherman's perspective, a naturalist's standpoint. Time now that we took to the air for a more sobering trip back upstream, an overflight of the half-million acre, 750-square-mile, bi-state, five-county watershed. The river, billed at the start of this book as among the region's "wildest and loveliest," is also something of an illusion.

The forested, marshy river and stream corridors are the exceptions, not the rule. Agriculture rules. Nearly half the land is cleared and plowed for fields of grain that feed more than half a billion chickens on Delmarva each year (some two hundred million in the Nanticoke drainage). From our aircraft, sun glints from the metal roofs of more than a thousand poultry houses sprinkled across the watershed, each hundreds of feet long, each producing some one hundred fifty thousand chickens a year—also hundreds of tons of manure.

Circular and semicircular patterns on cropland mark the heavy use of center-pivot irrigation, critical to wresting top yields from the region's drought-prone soils during the summer. Ironically, because the land is so flat and sluggish to drain, thousand of miles of ditches have been dug, and the majority of natural streams channelized and cleared of trees to whisk rain water away in winter and spring. Around Hollandsville in Kent County, ditching has actually cut through the natural watershed divide, joining the Nanticoke drainage with that of the Delaware Bay.

Forest accounts for about 40 percent of the Nanticoke basin, among the lowest tree coverage of all the sixty-two subbasins that make up the larger Chesapeake region. Away from the river, forests and wetlands are increasingly fragmented and isolated by farm fields, roads, and housing development, diminishing their habitat value for wildlife and effectiveness in absorbing polluted runoff. Many forests are commercial timberland, okay for water quality, but their pine monocultures are less diverse in wildlife.

Human development covers only around 4 percent of the watershed, but that is misleading. Everywhere the dominant pattern is sprawl, like pellets sprayed from a blunderbuss. The consequences are not just aesthetic. Each new person moving in uses on average double or triple the amount of land and energy (for commuting to work, school, shopping) that we did a few decades ago. The network of roads and power lines and commercial centers to serve such a spread-out population has further sliced and diced the natural landscape.

Our eagle's eye view also reveals a surprising acreage in the Nanticoke devoted to sand and gravel quarries, another consequence of serving

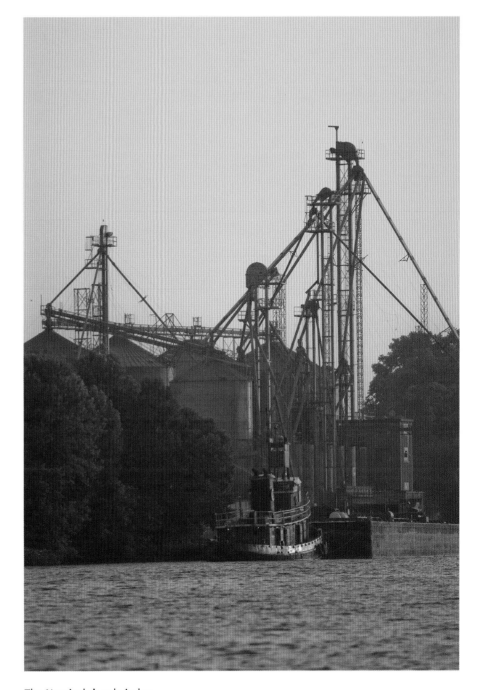

The Nanticoke's only industrial-commercial complex is at Seaford, a mix of grain elevators, chemical companies, and sand and gravel facilities.

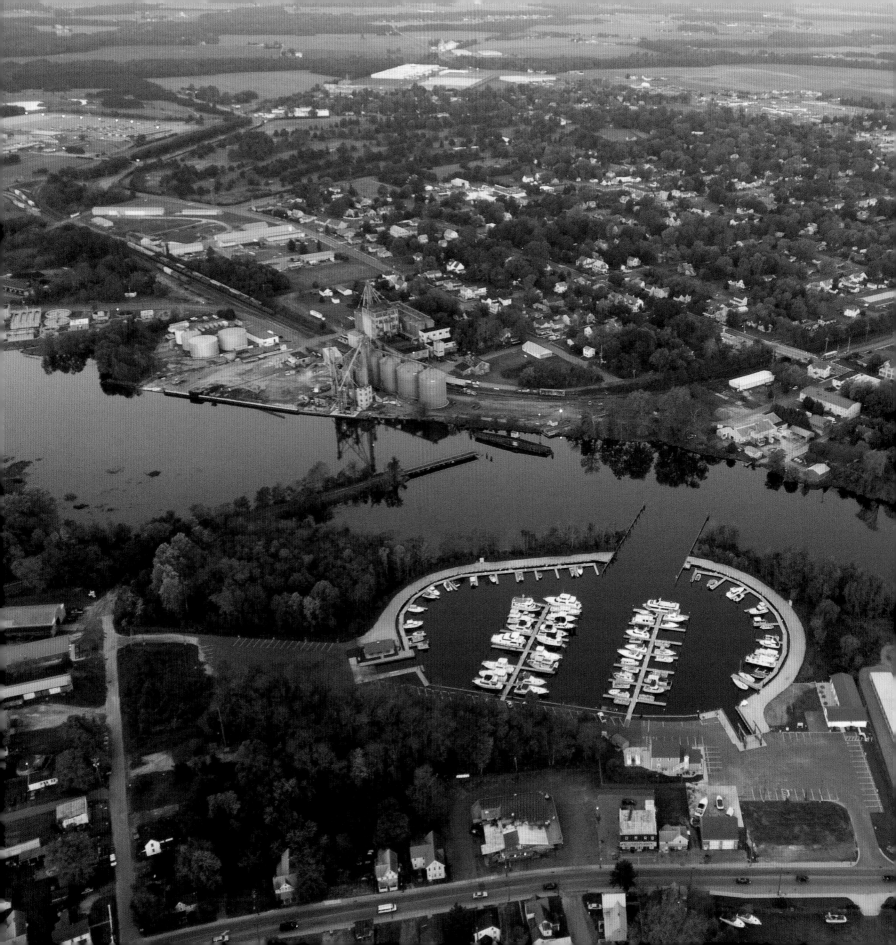

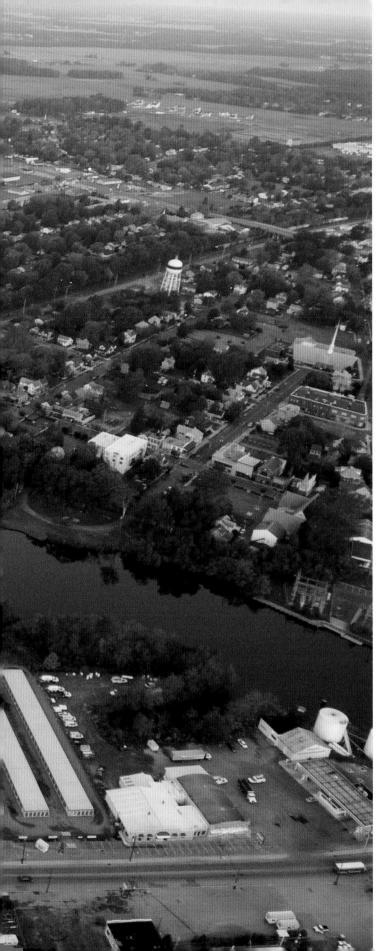

rapid development's need for concrete, parking lots, and highways. Also reflecting the trend to suburbia, open space is being turned into sod farms and nurseries growing azaleas, viburnums, and the like. These plants, grown under plastic, can create polluting stormwater runoff on the order of asphalted shopping centers.

I have made such overflights at different times with naturalists, farmers, commercial foresters, and realtors. Not surprisingly, each sees the landscape through a different lens, one's poison being another's pride.

But one thing all can agree: we are using the land harder than at anytime in history; asking two, three crops a year of the heavily fertilized farm fields, using genetic and nutritional wizardry to push evermore chickens through each chicken house, paving at a rate that has been rising five times faster than population, ratcheting

The new Blades marina, once an industrial site, holds pleasure craft across the river from Seaford.

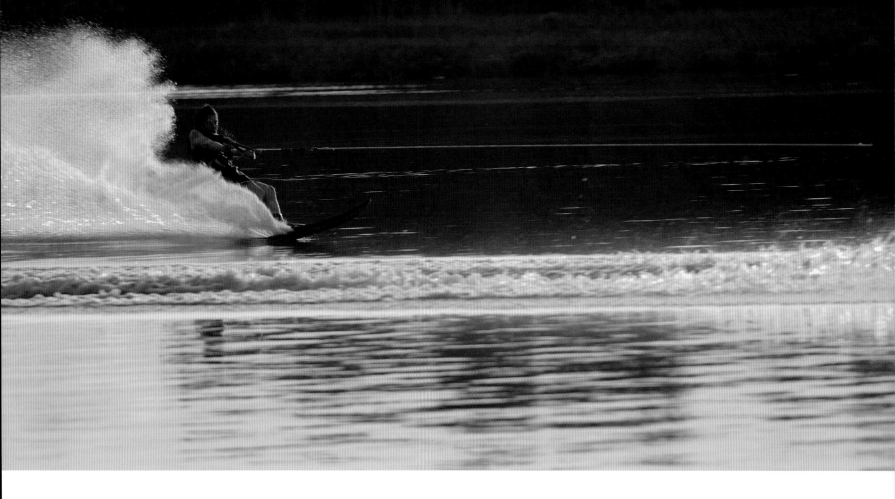

Alex Stek skims through summer on a long, straight reach of the main river.

up timber production per acre to offset a shrinking forest base.

So it is that while the literal view from the river is still just fine—even glorious—water quality and the natural landscape have been substantially degraded. Close to half the Nanticoke region, some two hundred thousand acres, was historically wetlands, supporting large and diverse numbers of plants and animals. Wetlands

are also natural filters for polluted runoff from farm fields, manure, pavement, and suburban lawns.

Nearly half the original wetlands are gone now. Of what remains, as much as 80 percent is severely to moderately degraded for habitat and water quality. Studies by the U.S. Fish and Wildlife Service and by both Maryland and Delaware have derived numerical values for eleven different indices of wetlands functions to show this; but the bottom line is what one Delaware biologist said: "basically, pretty screwed up."

All three major pollutants that are the target of the wider Chesapeake Bay restoration occur in the Nanticoke in spades. Nitrogen and phosphorus from agriculture, sewage, septic tanks, and stormwater runoff cause algae blooms that cloud the water and lower the oxygen needed by aquatic life. Sediment from fields and clearing for development further murk the water and smother oysters and gravel bottoms used by spawning fish.

Trends for all three of these pollutants during the past decade show no improvement (or worsening) in the Nanticoke. One bright note: nitrogen levels drop dramatically between Vienna and the Chesapeake, probably because the huge, meandering marshes where the Calloways fish are absorbing and converting this largest pollutant of the Bay to harmless nitrogen gas. But before celebrating, know that sea-level rise may submerge many of these wetlands in coming decades.

So what to do? Many will say we cannot stop the river and its drainage basin from changing, and they are half right. Over the centuries Delmarva's lands have yielded a constantly changing bounty—furs and tobacco, later wheat, fruit orchards, melons, strawberries, dairy, and tomatoes—these days, corn and soybeans and chickens.

Similarly the waters have furnished, in turn, sturgeon and caviar, diamondback terrapins, oysters, blue crabs, ducks for market gunners, later for sportsmen; from the forests, white cedar and cypress and oaks, now plantation pine for sawtimber, poles and pulp in paper making. Commercial watermen now are outnumbered by kayakers, canoeists, and pleasure boaters.

Constant change—but it has mostly been a *natural* progression, based on open, fertile lands, healthy waters, and undeveloped shorelines. We don't know to what uses a future Delmarva will put the lands and waters; but as long as we preserve this basic template of the past—keep our options open in other words—it's a fair bet the place will continue to provide food for both belly and soul, will retain the cultures and heritage that most residents say they value, over and over again, in polls.

As long as we keep our options open.

Consider agriculture, the largest source of water pollution and wetlands degradation across the Nanticoke watershed and much of Delmarva. There are proven and affordable techniques, like planting winter crops to absorb excess nitrogen, that could soon dramatically improve water quality; also planting forested buffers between fields and waterways to filter runoff; and plugging drainage ditches to create additional wetlands

almost overnight. The poultry industry has made a start in reducing the runoff of manure.

As much as we need to clean up agriculture, we equally need to keep farming viable, to keep the farmland option open. Because now we are faced with more fundamental change, the conversion of Delmarva into something more resembling Long Island. In just the past few decades, we have developed more open space across Delmarva than we did in the preceding few centuries, dating back to John Smith in 1608.

Sussex County, which contains the largest portion of the Nanticoke's watershed, has one of the fastest-growing populations in the United States—increasing 38 percent between 1990 and 2000, from 113,000 people to 156,000. By 2030 it is projected to hold 248,000 people.

Concepts like "livable Delaware" aim to minimize environmental impacts by focusing new building where the roads, sewage treat-

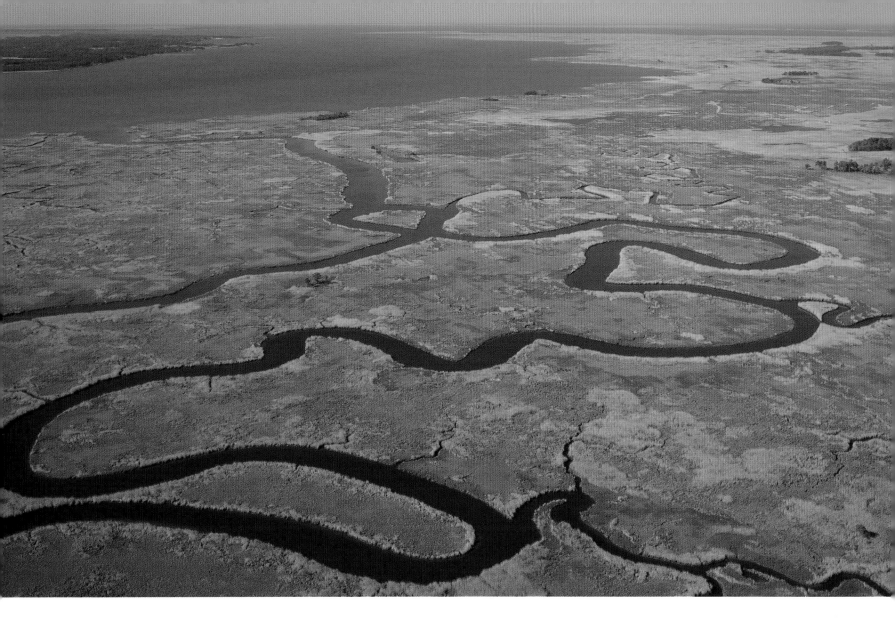

ment, and other facilities already support it, preserving farms, forests, and wetlands. But the reality is that Sussex County is wide open for development. If you equated excellent land use with Mount Everest, much of Delaware is nearer Death Valley. Over in the Maryland portions of the river, fast growing Wicomico and slower growing Dorchester counties look good only if compared with Sussex.

It does not have to be this way. Study after study confirms that allowing sprawl leads to higher taxes as well as to heavy environmental costs. More restrictive zoning seldom devalues private property because open space is becoming such a sought-after amenity.

Both states have programs to preserve farm-land and open space that could be better funded and better focused on the Nanticoke; and a num-

Beard Creek and Bozes Creek converge into Jacks Creek and the lower Nanti-coke, taking their time to get there.

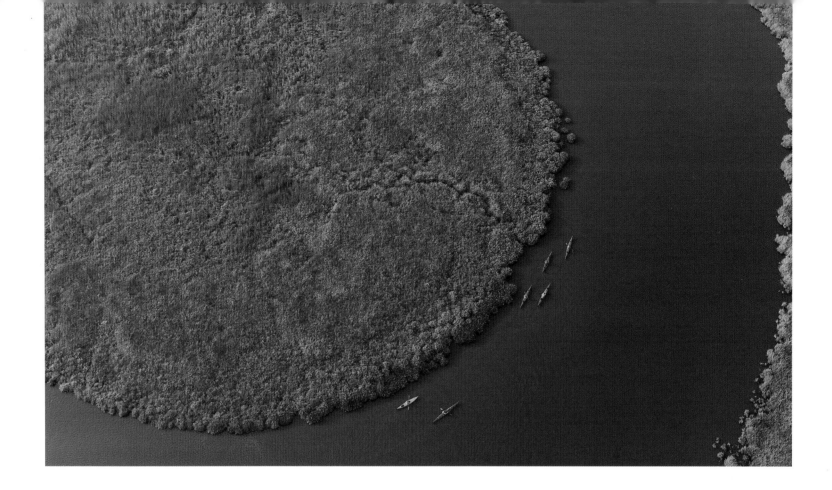

Sea kayaks round one of Barren Creek's many curves on their way upstream to Mardela Springs.

ber of private land conservation groups like the Conservation Fund and the Nature Conservancy are active in the region. Supporting local land trusts, like the Eastern Shore Land Conservancy and the Lower Shore Land Trust, to complement these should be a high priority.

It is especially prudent to protect the shorelines throughout the tidal Nanticoke from more development, given their huge habitat values for spawning fish and turtles and for other wildlife. Also, because of the inevitability of sea-level rise, leaving the shorelines open—again, maintaining options—would allow space for future wetlands

to form and prevent costly public bailouts of low-lying development.

On the Nanticoke there's still time to do it right. The option is ours—a river and a landscape that will change, inevitably, but most likely in ways reflecting Delmarva's rural heritage and cultures—or something fundamentally different, depressingly like the soulless suburban landscapes that increasingly surround the peninsula.

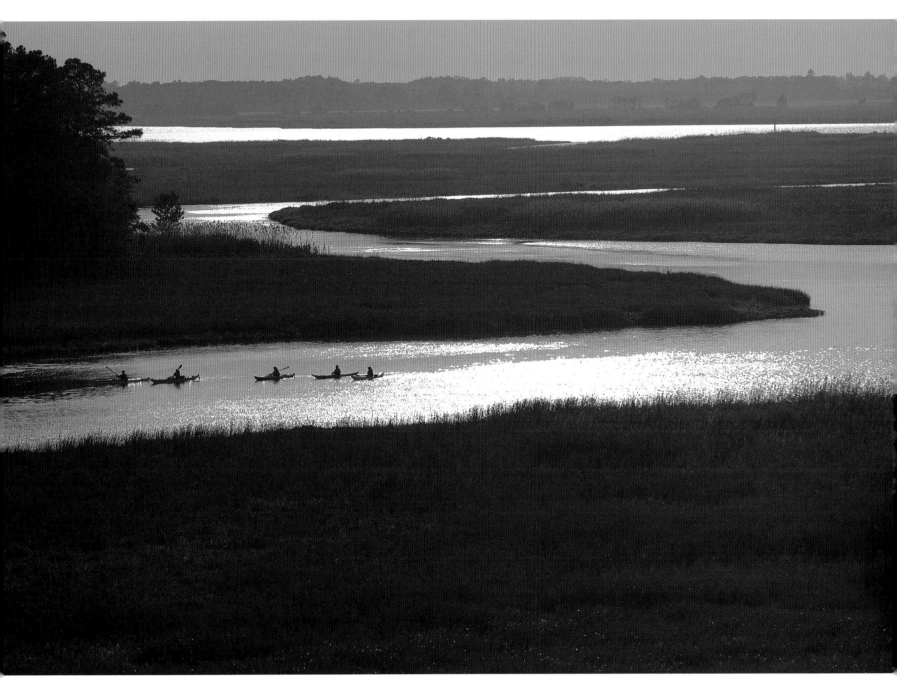

Above: Late afternoon sun glints on Barren Creek, with the main Nanticoke in the background.

Overleaf: Hibiscus light up the marshes by the U.S. 50 bridge. Water Street in Vienna is across the river.

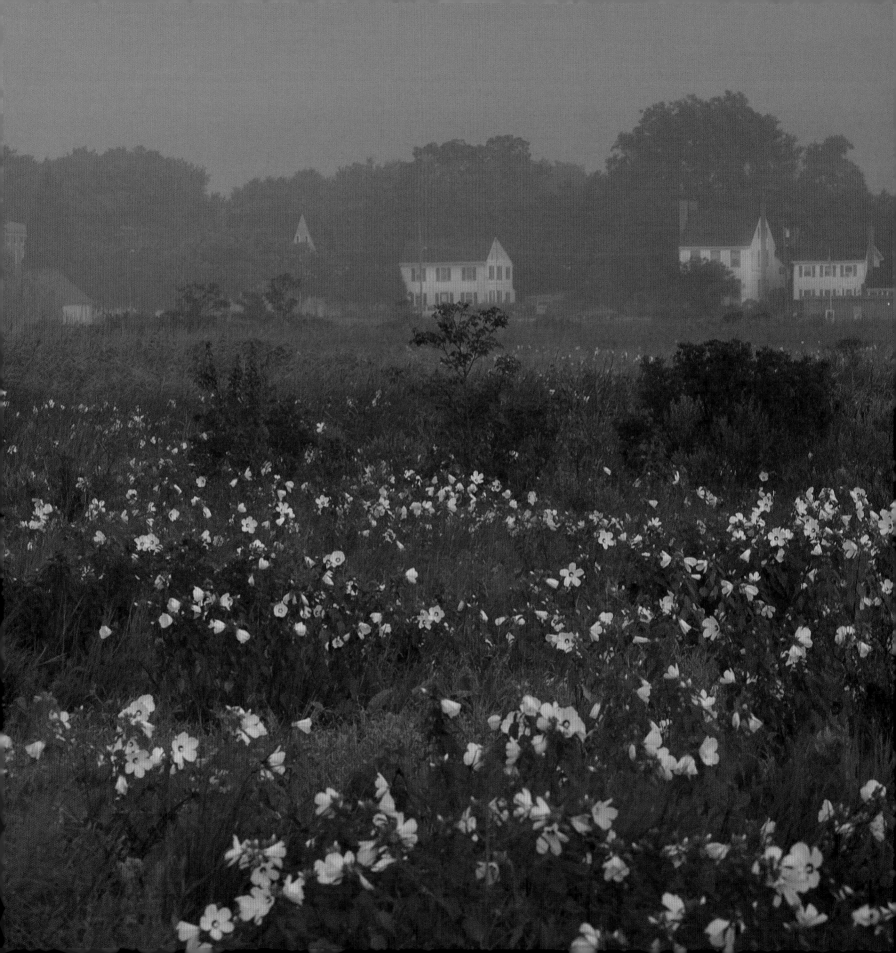

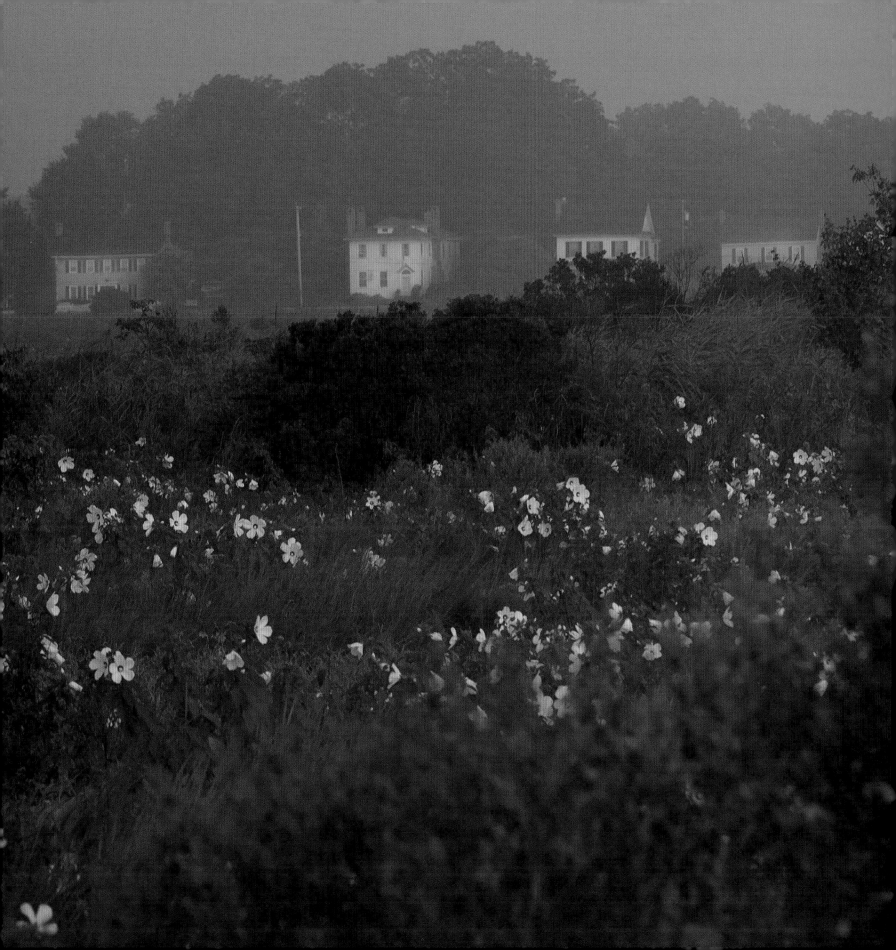

Tickseed sunflowers in autumn blanket the marshes where U.S. 50 crosses at Vienna.

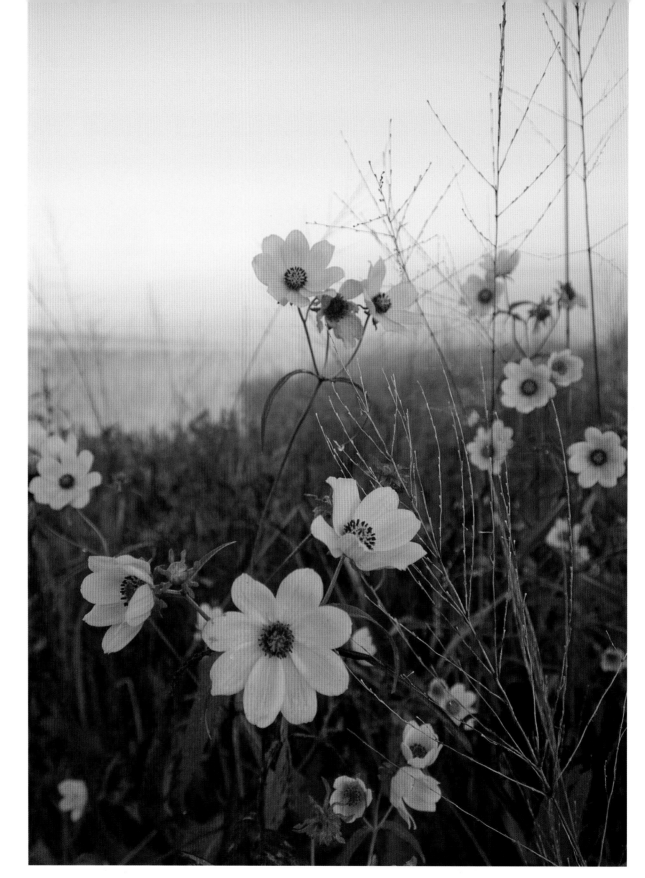

400 YEARS

Ed Haile watches a leaf sweep by on the ebb tide gurgling down the Nanticoke River: "Hard to imagine they could have moved that far and fast against such a current," he says.

It's a bright, still June morning on the river, almost four centuries to the week since Captain John Smith and his crew of a dozen Jamestown colonists entered the Nanticoke on their historic, 1608 exploration that first mapped the Chesapeake Bay.

Launching from Vienna by the U.S. 50 bridge and heading upstream for Delaware, we've assembled our own crew—historians, archaeologists, computer mapping experts, mariners, and river rats to explore a high-stakes mystery.

Among our guides are a reproduction of Smith's map, first published in 1612; also a new map of the Bay and its rivers from the National Geographic Society. It's testament to the English explorer how much his ancient Nanticoke

resembles the latest, satellite-derived version, rendered as it was with only compass, crude sextant, hourglass, and no knowledge of longitude (east-west position).

The Geographic's map depicts in unbroken blue lines the full extent of Smith's 2,500-mile journey throughout the Chesapeake and its major rivers. Only a careful reader might notice that where the Nanticoke forks above Vienna, with the main river going toward Seaford, Delaware, and a substantial branch heading off toward Federalsburg, Maryland, even the Society's experts were puzzled. A dotted blue line shows "possible route" for some twelve to fifteen miles up the Marshy Hope Creek toward Federalsburg.

And one might ask, at this late date, "so what?" There's an obligation to history, of course, to get it right. But it's the river's—and the Chesapeake's—future that's got four boatloads of us out here today, floating beneath fluffy clouds and high-

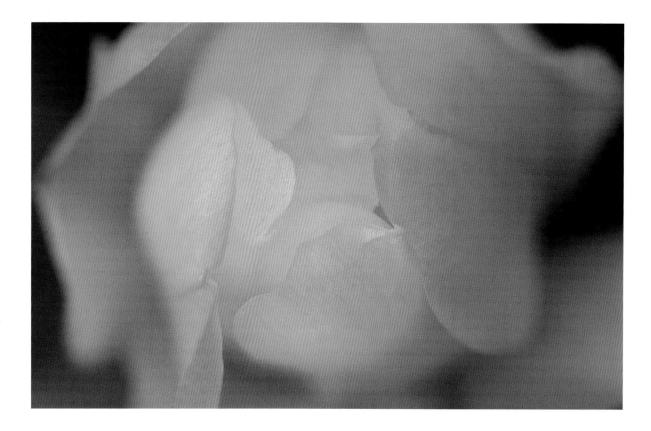

Light glows through a prickly pear cactus flower.

flying eagles at the swampy, forested confluence of Nanticoke and Marshy Hope, arguing heatedly over which way Smith turned all those years ago —also daring to wonder, did he get this far at all?

His stubby little shallop, an open barge about thirty feet long, propelled by sail and oars, was heavy and slow. The Nanticoke represented his deepest penetration into Delmarva, but he spent less than two days in the river before heading for the Western Shore, and he entered with the ebb tide against him.

It's important to know which way the captain turned here at the confluence. The United States Congress is considering a unique national park— a Captain John Smith National Historic Water Trail around the Bay. It would bring ecotourism to the river—and quite likely much more.

It has great potential, like the Appalachian Trail on land, to catalyze a water trail stretching ultimately the length of the East Coast; it also has the potential to become a vehicle for protecting from development large sections of the Nanticoke and Chesapeake landscape for public access and to preserve unspoiled views such as those Smith described in 1608.

It also faces formidable odds in a Congress and an administration that has been loath to

A wild sunflower reflects in Big Creek.

establish any new parks. The trail's backers need to add Delaware's congressional clout to that of Maryland and Virginia—which is to say it'd be nice to establish that Smith did turn toward Seaford, as his map seems to indicate (a cross around what may be Broad Creek in Delaware marks the extent of his exploration of the river).

The town of Vienna also has a lot riding on what we conclude. Like all the Nanticoke's small towns, it is struggling to revitalize its core amid a sea of suburban sprawl that has sucked the money and the life out of traditional downtowns. It has big plans for a John Smith interpretive center to draw tourists. Little Vienna, population around 280, not much changed since 1706, has hired Michael Scott, a computer mapping specialist from Salisbury University, to establish whether Smith went ashore at or near the town.

Scott, who's with us today, employed a technique known as "rubber sheeting," overlaying Smith's map of the Nanticoke with modern maps, then attempting to "tug" the two into an approximate fit on his computer. The task increased his admiration for Smith's mapping: "to do as well as he did was incredibly difficult." He feels certain, Scott says, that the Nanticoke king's village of "Kuskarawaok," where Smith likely visited, lay close by present-day Vienna.

Not so fast, counters Wayne Clark, a respected

archaeologist with the Maryland Historical Trust who's in our flotilla today. Based on known sites of Nanticoke Indian villages and his reading of Smith's map, Clark puts Kuskarawaok miles upstream of Vienna, where the Marshy Hope Creek wends through Maryland. Federalsburg sees this as its opportunity to seize on the John Smith quadracentennial to revitalize itself.

Smith's map, so recognizable even today from the Nanticoke's mouth to above Vienna, gets funky above the confluence. To further complicate things, Beth Ragan, a local archaeologist, notes that the Native Americans by Smith's time had been planting corn for hundreds of years, moving their villages as the soil wore out. Over the centuries, they probably inhabited every piece of suitable high ground up and down the river, she says.

Then there's the bigger question: how did Smith, in such a short time with such a ponder-

ous craft, manage to get dozens of miles up the river to either Delaware or the Marshy Hope?

One of our crew, a seasoned boater of Chesapeake rivers, ventures that Smith was "either a helluva man or a helluva liar." Indeed, a forthcoming modern history of Smith's explorations hedges on the issue: "It is uncertain just how far up the Nanticoke River Smith and his men explored…Smith may instead have relied on information supplied by the local inhabitants." (We know the Indians could draw accurate maps and that Smith was good at eliciting information from them.)

But Clark thinks Smith could have parked the shallop and hitchhiked. Smith's journal, which treats the Nanticoke only briefly, mentions: "we became such friends (with the natives) that they would contend who should fetch us water, stay with us for hostage, *conduct our men any whither*" (emphasis added). In other words, Clark

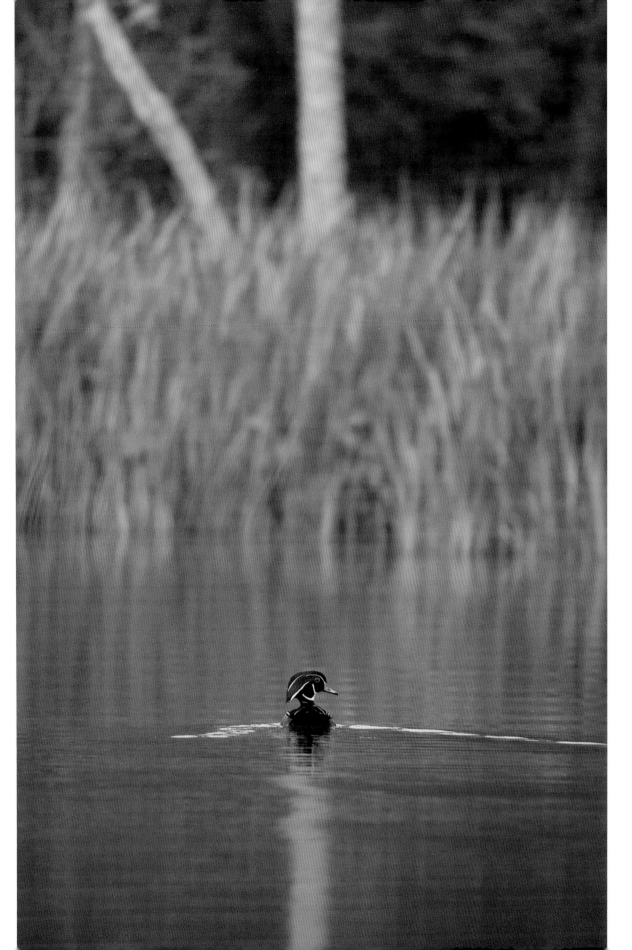

A drake wood duck patrols on Owens Branch, protected by the Nature Conservancy. Male "woodies" are among the Bay's most colorful waterfowl. Hunters and conservationists erect nesting boxes on poles to boost wood duck numbers.

contends, Smith's men were taken in Indian dugout canoes, which reached fifty feet in length. Manned by as many as twenty paddlers, they could have swept far upriver and down with relative ease.

Clark further argues that Smith, never mind whether he was inclined to follow the main Nanticoke into Delaware, would have been taken where the Indians wanted to take him, to a major village upriver towards Federalsburg.

The evidence for a major Indian village up the Marshy Hope is more than just archaeological. It's apparent everywhere you look—great, green swaths of aquatic plants along the banks, their roots and tubers rich in starches, made this section of the river a breadbasket. Here too, were the spawning grounds for great spring runs of striped bass, herring, and shad. The Marshy Hope was so rich in beaver and other mammals that it was one of the last areas of the Delmarva Peninsula where

colonial governments—avid for furs the Indians trapped—allowed settlers to push the natives out. It is no coincidence that today's resurgence of beaver along the river is greatest along these same stretches.

But all of this applies equally to the main stem of the river going up to Broad Creek in Delaware.

We reached no conclusion on Smith's route that day, but many months later the consensus is clear. On a perfect May morning, a crowd of more than two hundred assembles at Phillips Landing at the mouth of Broad Creek to unveil a handsome granite monument commemorating Smith's journey up the Nanticoke into Delaware.

The Captain John Smith National Historic Water Trail, the first national park of its kind, more than two thousand miles long, is a reality. President George W. Bush signed it into law on December 19, 2006, four centuries to the day since Smith sailed from England. Conservation-

Opposite: Welcome back—four hundred years after Captain John Smith sailed his shallop around the Chesapeake, a recreation of his historic mapping expedition plies a Nanticoke the captain might still recognize.

ists are already at work with Delaware to protect a large tract of choice wetlands and forests just upstream as part of the new trail.

And something else, both new and old, is afloat on the river this dedication day: John Smith's shallop, or rather a reproduction of it, bobs gently at the Landing as people line up to speak to its crew of volunteers. Fourteen young men and women are rowing and sailing it throughout the Chesapeake, following the captain's four-hundred-year-old tracks.

One almost hesitates to ask Ian Bystrom, the captain, but does he think Smith during his short time on the river could possibly have made it this far on his crews' own power?

The boat is slow, Bystrom confirms, and the tide was against them almost from the mouth to above Vienna. But rowing and sailing, they took about ten hours to come here from the lower Nanticoke. "Did Smith do it?" he muses. "It is certainly possible. We have proven that."

The most memorable feature of that historic day on the Nanticoke was not the new national park, not the shallop, nor the hoopla over John Smith that brought Queen Elizabeth of England to the Bay that summer to celebrate the old seadog's four hundredth.

It was an erect, bronzed man in fringed deerskin leggings and full, feathered headdress, with a breastplate of shell and bone. He stood on the dais next to Delaware's top elected officials and was the first to speak. He began, not in his native language, which was lost more than 150 years ago, but in Algonquian:

"To you, good morning. I am a Nanticoke man, chief of the Nanticoke people, Chief Tidewater Laughing Wolf. Peace."

Most of my life I heard there were no Indians. As a boy on the Nanticoke more than fifty years ago I knew the Indian names were all around—Big Indian Creek, Indiantown road, Chicone, Rewastico, Quantico, Manumsco, Wetipquin,

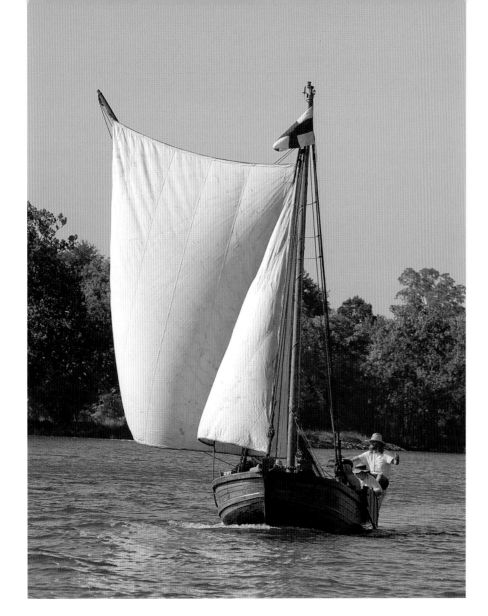

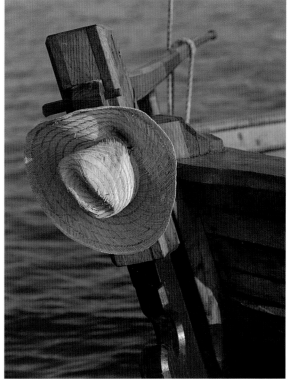

Tyaskin. But no Indians. I was assured they had vanished long ago.

Official records in Maryland and Delaware then classed folks as "white," "black," or "other." Anyhow, "there was no percentage advertising you were an Indian," a short, rotund man with flowing grey locks standing next to me at the dedication said. He was Sewell Fitzhugh, also Winterhawk, Chief of the Nause-Waiwash Band of Indians, descended from native peoples living in the Dorchester county marshes of the lower Nanticoke. Smith identified Nause on his map, and archaeologists have uncovered its location recently.

"In the sixth grade I was run down, beat on, peed on in the street," Winterhawk recalled. "My daughter in the eighth grade was told by a boy, 'I'd like to f—— you 'cause I've never had an Indian.'"

"I do a lot of school appearances these days,"

Captain Ian Bystrom and a crew of twelve men and women sailed nearly 1,700 miles in the summer of 2007.

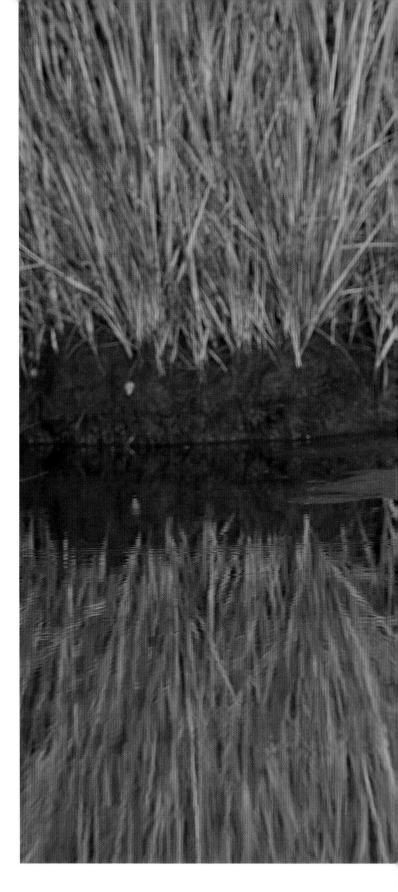

An immature green heron progues for dinner amid spartina grasses of the lower river.

Winterhawk laughs. "I always get someone says 'I thought we killed all of you,' and I say, no, you missed a few."

The Nanticoke, scholars think, numbered perhaps two hundred warriors and their families in 1608. By century's end they were already hard-pressed by settlers moving into their traditional territories. By the early 1700s they were confined to three reservations, near Vienna, up the Marshy Hope, and along Broad Creek near present-day Laurel. By the late 1700s, most had disbanded, traveling north and west to assimilate into other tribes as far away as Canada.

But a few remained. Scattering along the Eastern Shore's streams and rivers, on the edges of the swamps, deep in the piney woods, known only to one another, they endured.

"We survived by living to an extent like Amish, socializing among ourselves, marrying within our community, putting a premium on owning land,

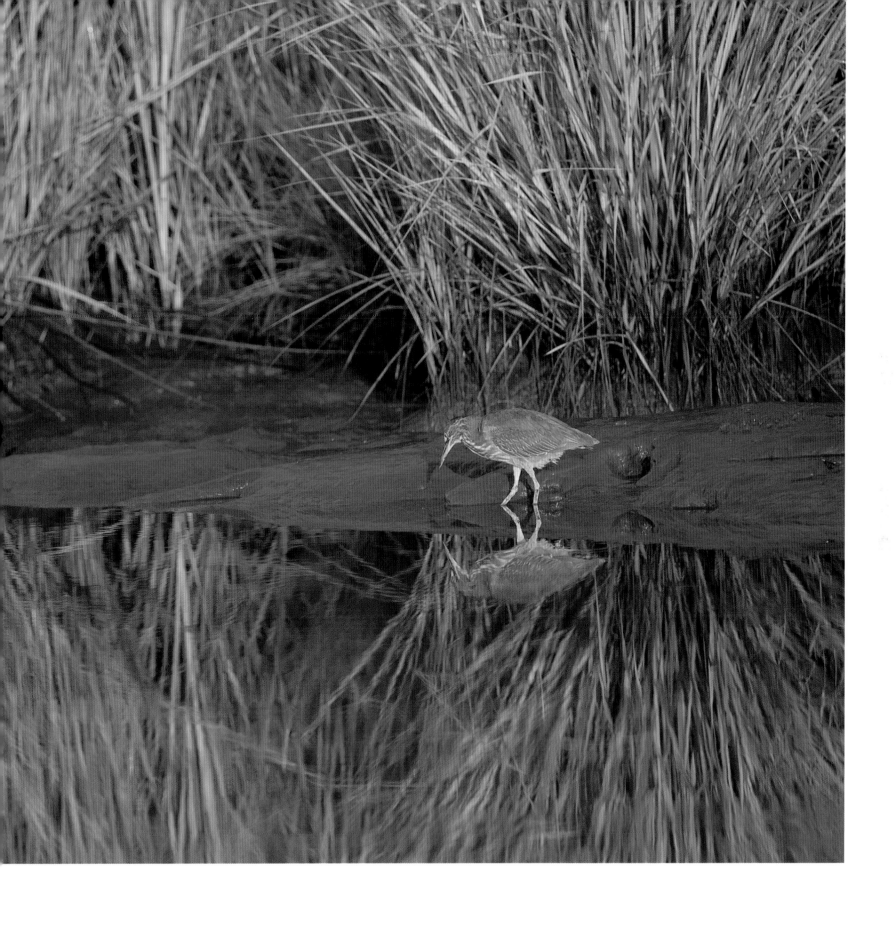

starting our own elementary school," explained Laughing Wolf, also known as James "Tee" Norwood.

He and his wife, Princess Laughing Water, are both retired Verizon employees. Some Nanticoke families, like his wife's, refused to send their children to black schools, preferring the federal Indian school, Haskell Institute, in Lawrence, Kansas, the chief said.

In recent decades there's been a resurgence of interest. Nanticoke powwows annually draw tens of thousands of people to near Millsboro, Delaware. There's a Nanticoke Museum and a Nanticoke community center nearby. The tribe, officially recognized by Delaware, has about a thousand members. While no full-blooded Indians remain, a tribal integrity clearly has been maintained through the centuries.

The Nause-Waiwash in Maryland, their history less well-documented, are still petitioning for state recognition. Chief Winterhawk's group numbers a few hundred members and growing, as people rediscover their identities.

"I'd grown up hearing old family stories about Indian ancestors and never much believed 'em," said Jeff Kirwan, a tribal member and forestry professor at Virginia Tech who grew up in Dorchester County. "Then I began finding the same stories had come down to other families unrelated to us. I found an old dugout canoe on some marsh I own, and I thought, there's something to this."

Ironically, the Delaware Nanticoke's future may be less secure than ever, Laughing Wolf says: "Desegregation was a gain for society, but a setback to maintaining our tribal identity; we are glad to see it, but these days it's more important for our kids to get to the high school ball game than a tribal event."

The John Smith Quadracentennial has come

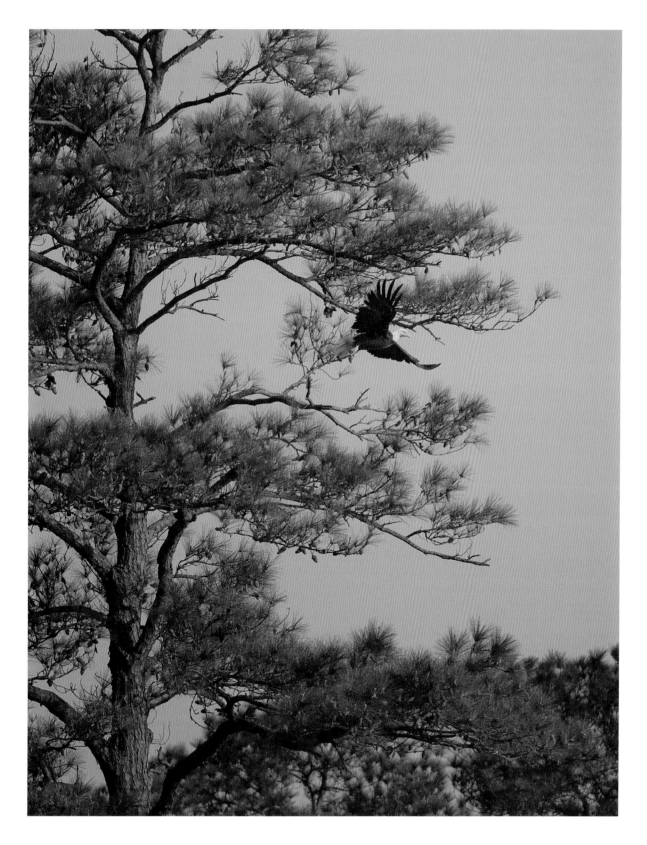

A bald eagle perches in a loblolly pine—two icons of the Nanticoke.

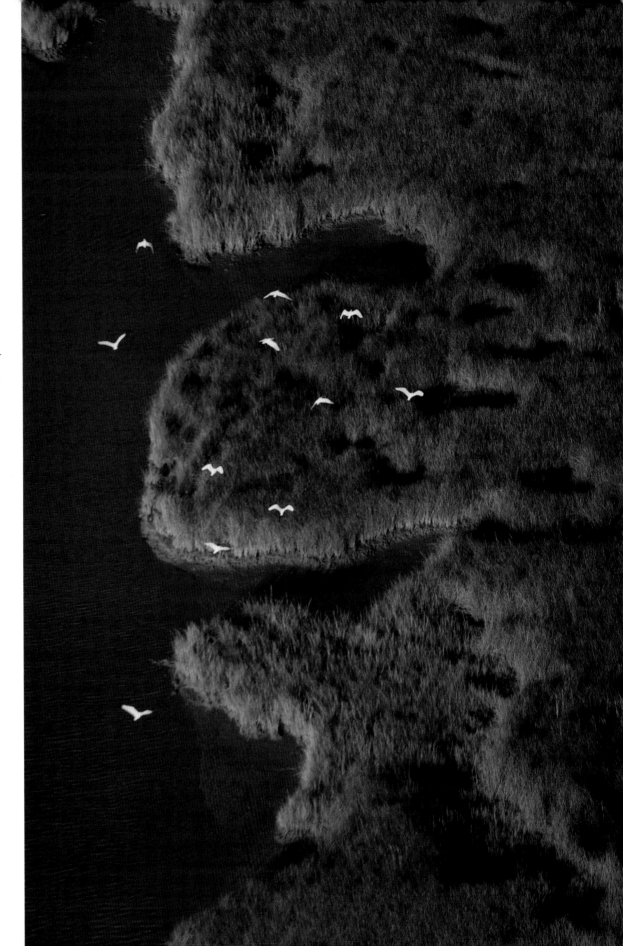

Egrets ornament an interior marsh around Savanna Lake off the Elliott's Island road.

and gone. The real work has just begun—using the new national water trail to protect precious natural resources threatened by rampant development along the Nanticoke and throughout the Chesapeake. In that respect, we'd all do well to learn something about Indian values.

A developer approached him recently with promises of a chiefly sum to acquire his forty-eight-acre farm for tract housing, Chief Laughing Wolf says. The man was astounded when the chief said he wasn't interested at any price.

"You don't even want to hear my offer?" the developer said. Replied the chief: "It just wouldn't matter; you can't buy my peace."

Sticklers may note that all the above hasn't answered the mystery—where John Smith really traveled on the Nanticoke. I would submit that we may never know conclusively, and that it isn't what's important.

Smith's explorations themselves were a failure of sorts. He was to find the northwest passage to Asia, send home to England precious metals and gemstones, and he did none of this—merely played a critical role in establishing what would become the United States of America.

If Smith's era was one of exploration and exploitation, ours more and more needs to become the era of restoration, protecting, revitalizing, rebuilding the fabulous, beleaguered, natural heritage of the nation.

On the Nanticoke, in the Chesapeake, up and down the East Coast, the new John Smith water trail can play a role in that, and not by choosing between Marshy Hope or main Nanticoke, between Maryland or Delaware—rather by making us see the Bay, its rivers, and the 64,000 square miles of land they drain as a seamless whole, not a single square inch disconnected in its fate from all the rest.

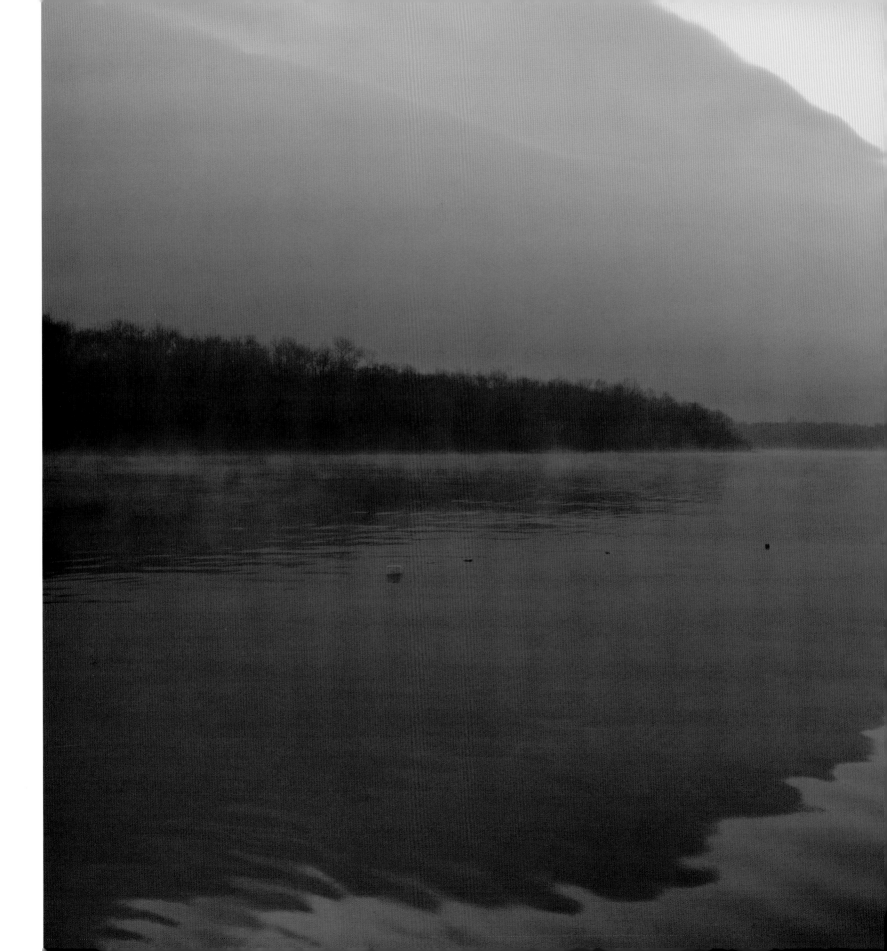

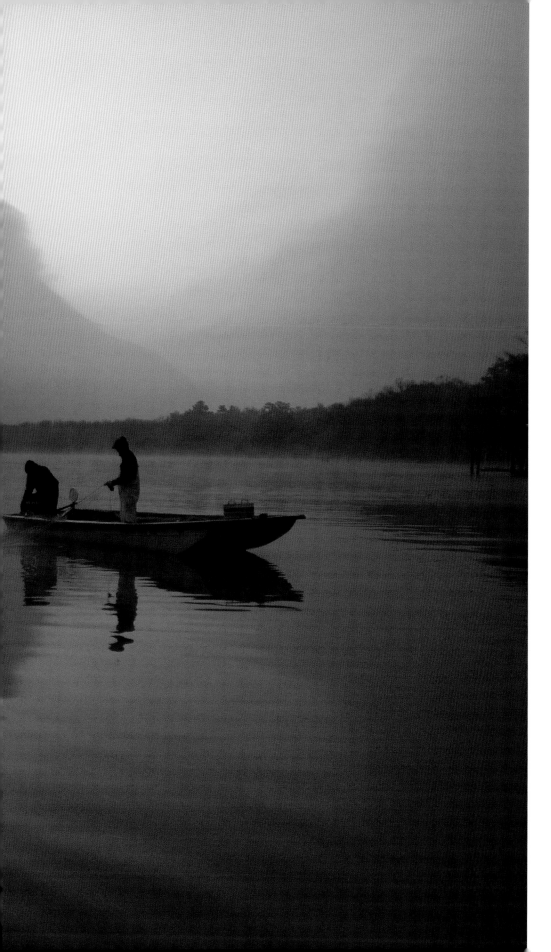

An April cold front moves across the Marshy Hope Creek at Brookview, where Fred Harrison, nowadays with son Clark, has netted shad and herring for fifty years.

Clark Harrison sets a gill net
in the cool spring waters of
Marshy Hope Creek.

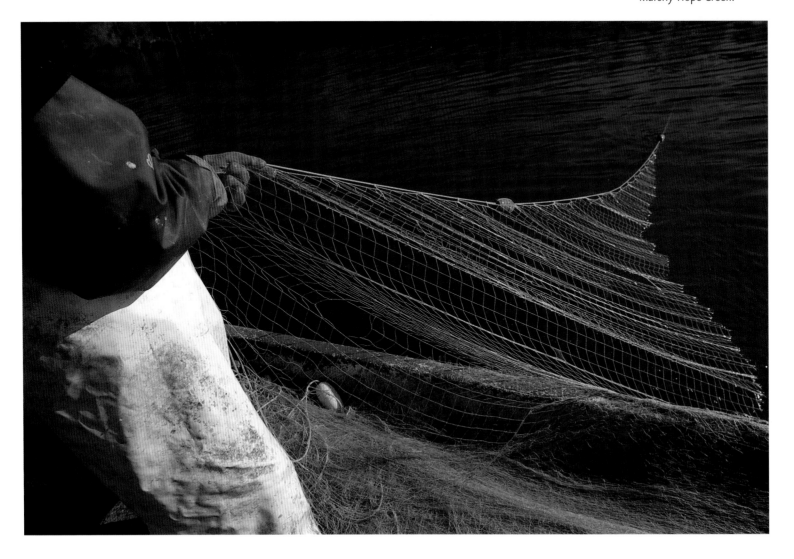

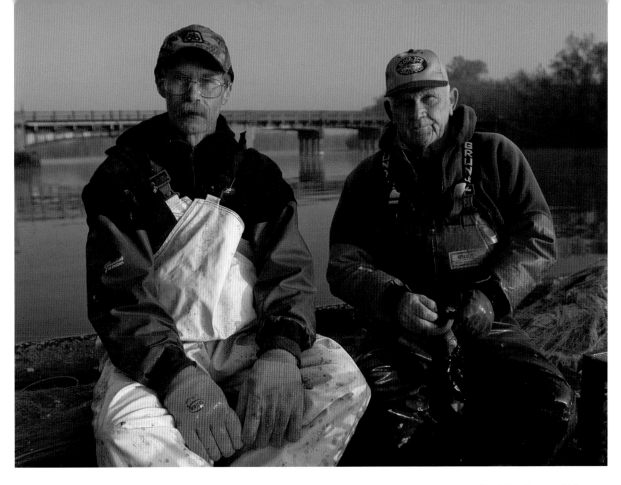

Fred Harrison and his son, Clark, use a gill net to catch herring near the Brookview Bridge on Marshy Hope Creek.

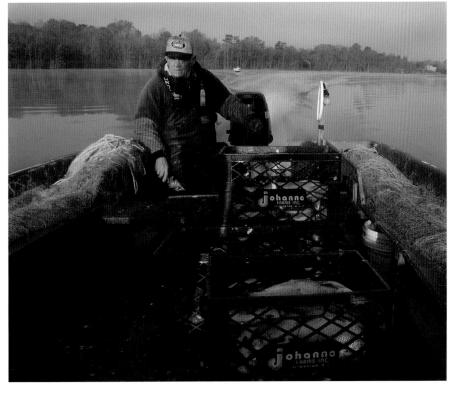

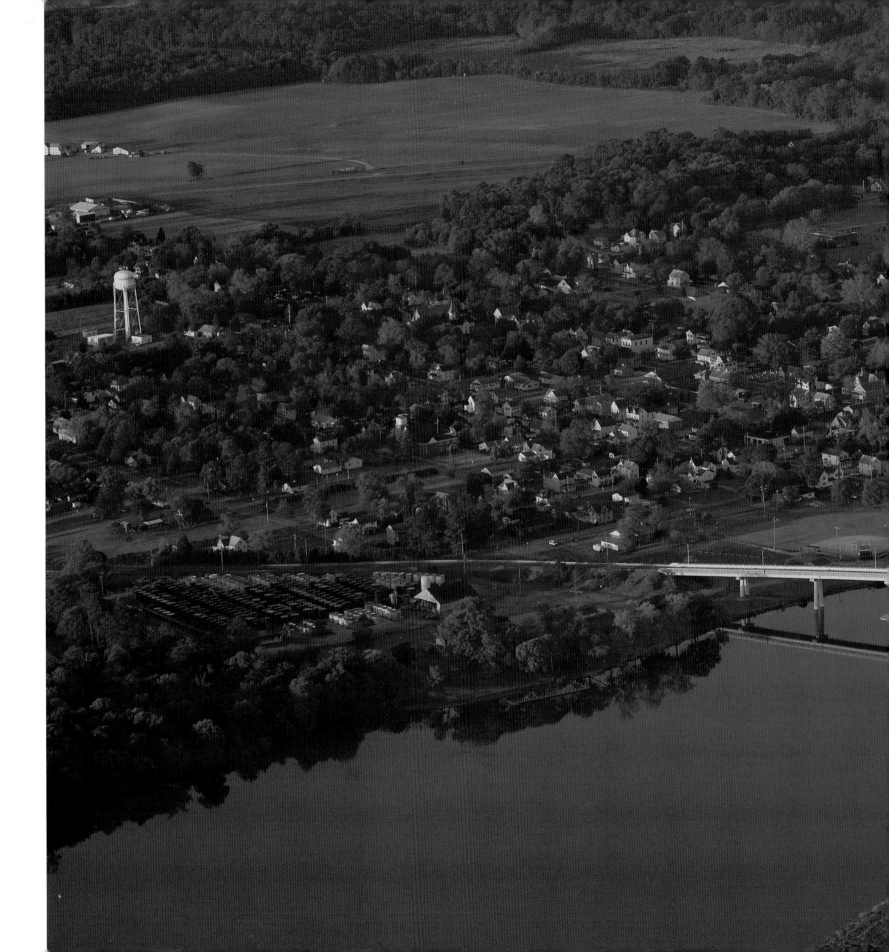

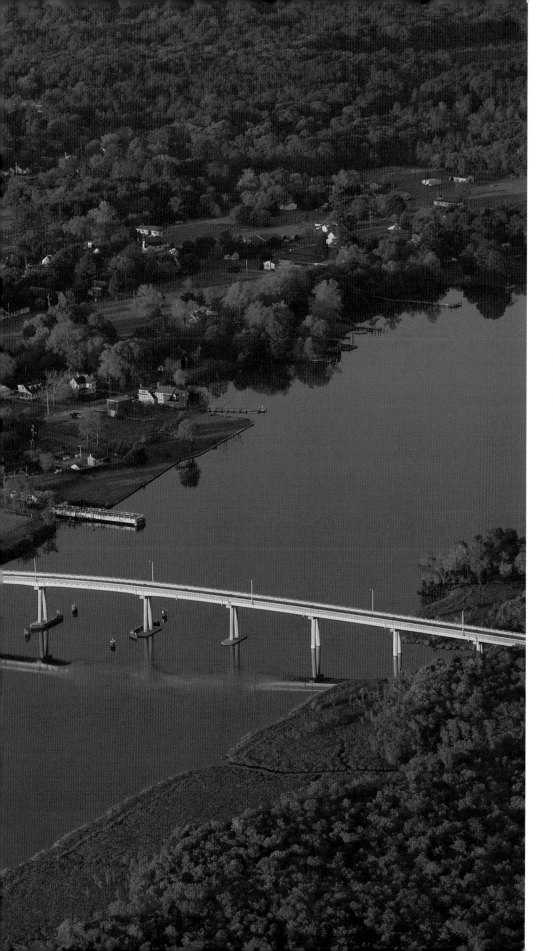

Sharptown, one of the river's larger communities, is an historic center of fishing and boat building.

Overleaf: One of the Bay region's sweet spots—the confluence of Marshy Hope and Nanticoke reflects the sun of an autumn morning.

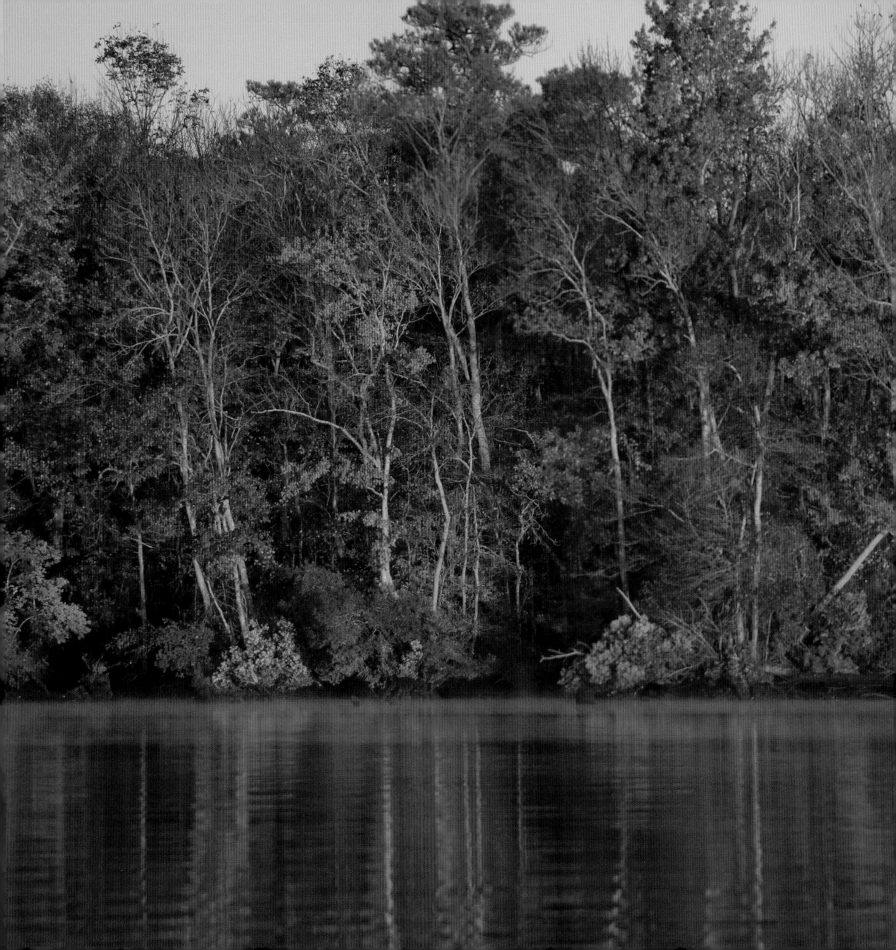

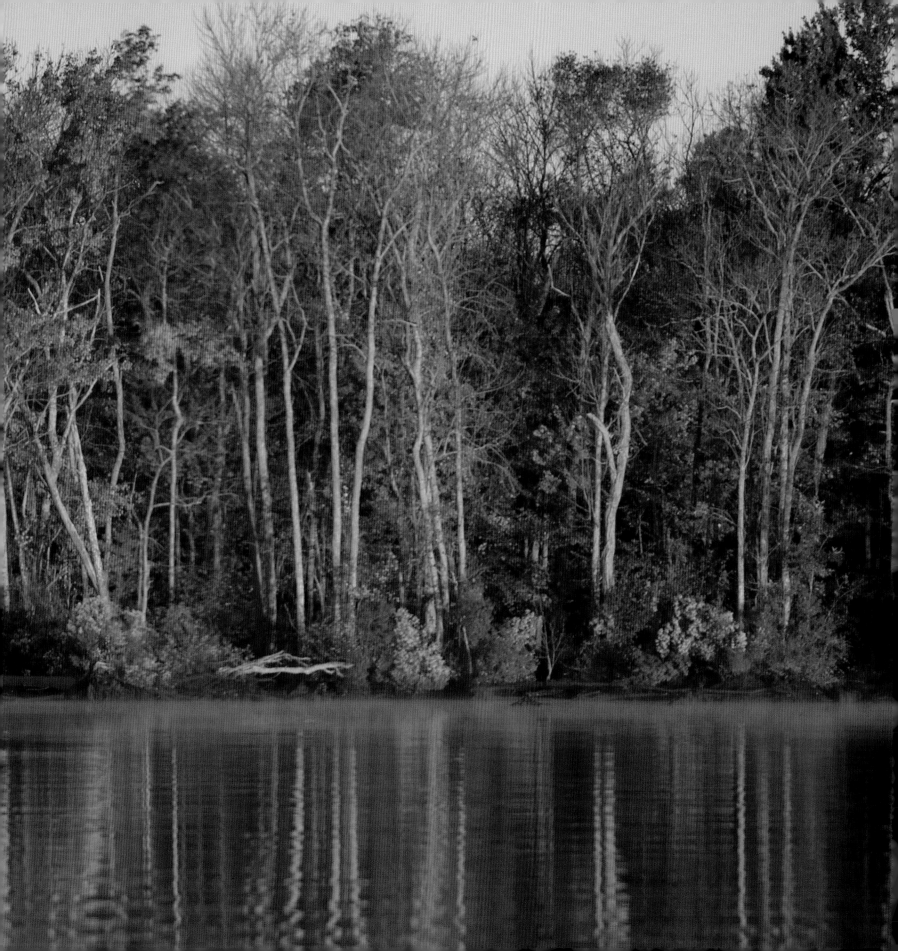

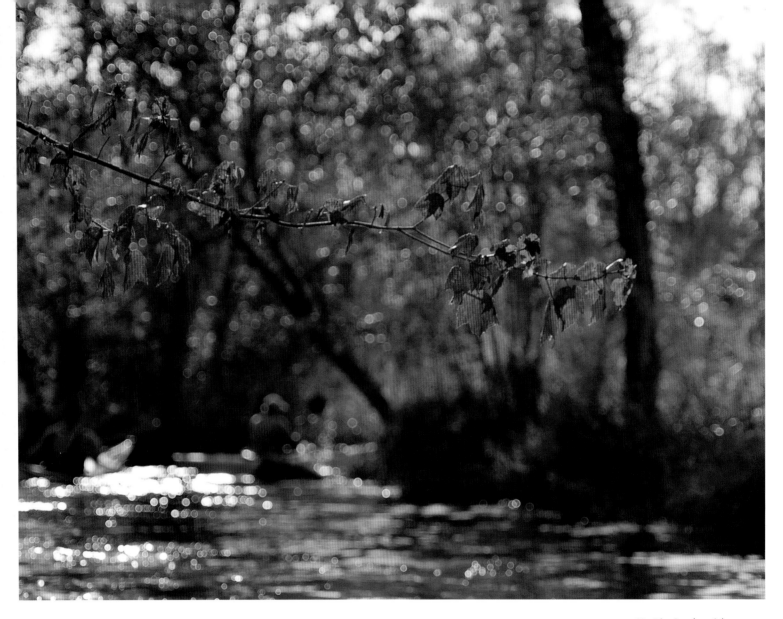

Up Big Creek, with a
paddle. Kayakers can follow
this canopied watercourse
for miles, from around
Walnut Landing to where it
emerges again well below
Riverton.

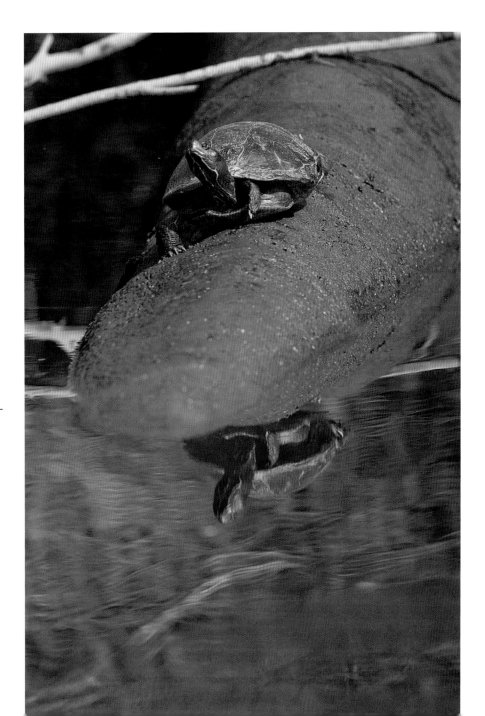

A turtle goes on alert as a passing kayak spoils its sun-bath on Broad Creek.

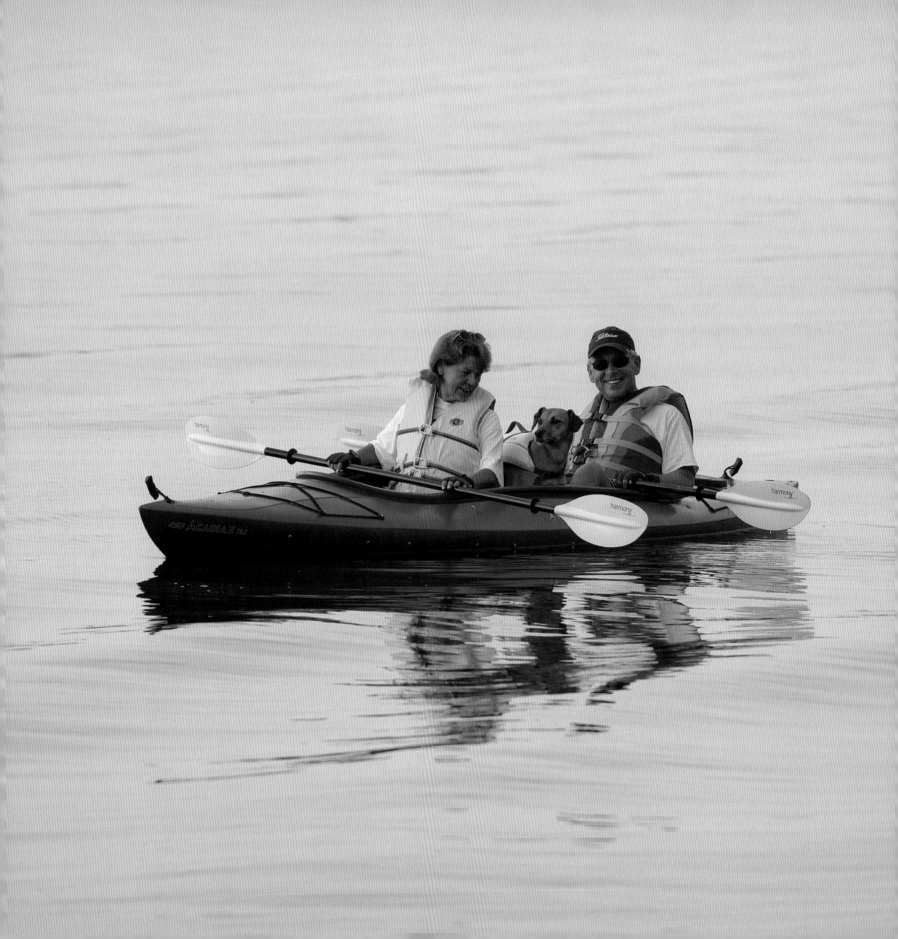

RIVER TIME

We launched in T-shirts, swatting mosquitoes in Seaford; landed three days later to the music of swans riding a cold nor'wester across the Elliott's Island marshes.

If there was a point to the trip on which our small flotilla of Nanticoke kayakers embarked one early December, it lay somewhere between Chesapeake singer Tom Wisner's lyrics...

Hey there, wild river, teach me to flow
Tell me your poems and all the songs that you know

and Langston Hughes's river poem:

I bathed in the Euphrates when the dawns were young.
I built my hut near the Congo and it lulled me to sleep.
I looked upon the Nile and raised the pyramids above it

In my traveling days I floated a rude canoe on the Nile at Khartoum and watched a young Sudanese woman trudge the river shore, bent like a pack animal beneath a load of firewood. She set it down and for a few moments pranced like a child in the rich, glistening mud of the river's floodplain.

And now, thirty years later—three thousand years it could be—a young girl in our band of paddlers frolics on Nanticoke mudflats, delighted by her footprints in the dark, shining slate exposed by low tide.

Long freed by technology of any need to live by rivers for drinking, washing, fishing, and transportation, we remain wedded to flowing water. From associations as old as the human race, rivers run through our being.

Three days by kayak is about right for seeing a good section of the Nanticoke, from cozy, headwater streams to prairie-like salt marshes. It's about right, too, for settling into river time, letting tide and wind and what lies around the next bend or up a creeky detour dictate the pace.

Early on, two of our band lag back. They're not

Opposite: Rob and Nancy Heflin, out for a spin in front of their home on Cow Island in the Nanticoke, never go on kayak journeys without their beloved Maggie.

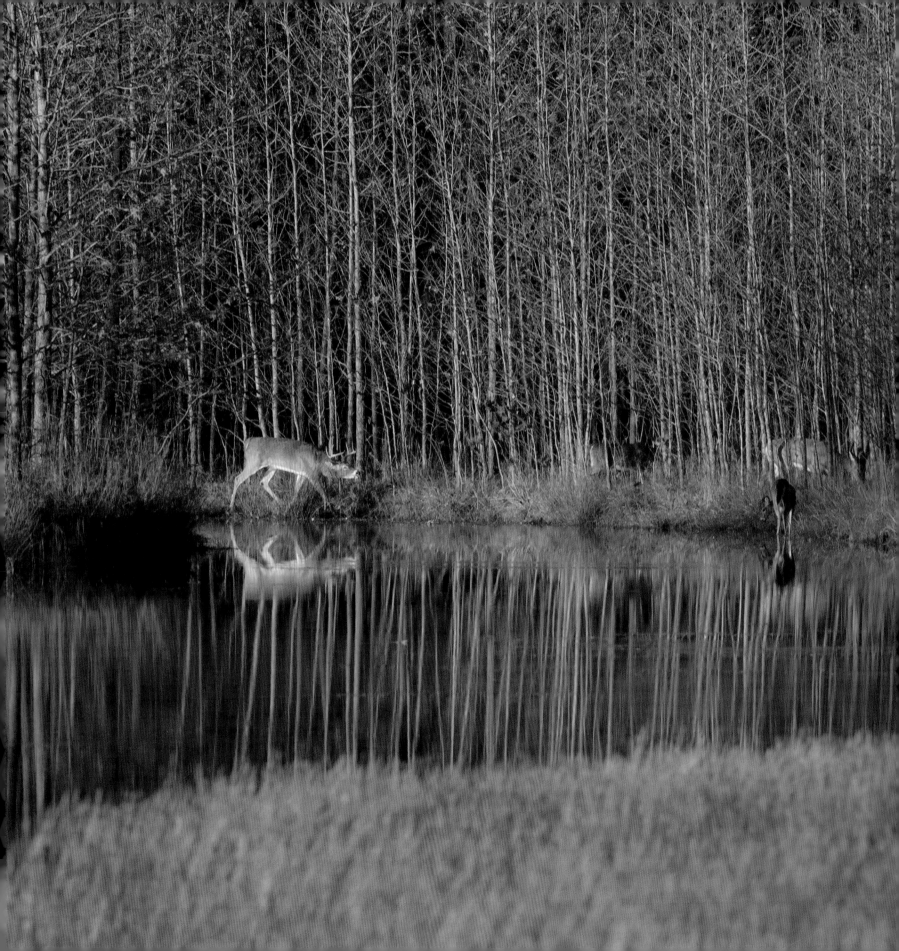

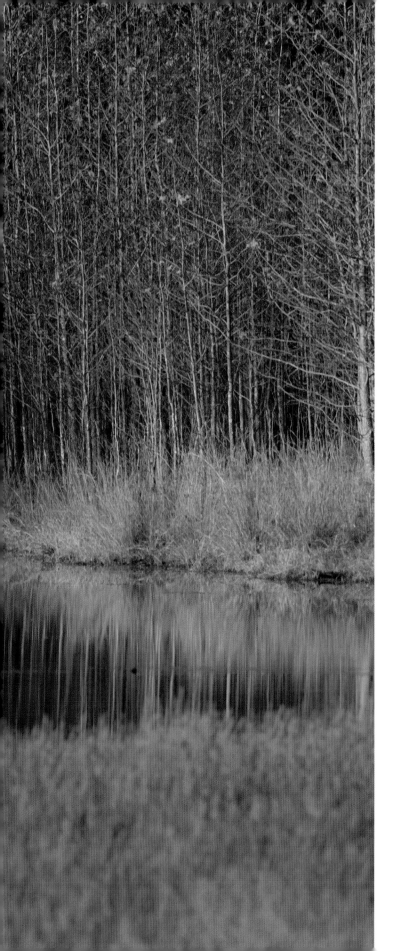

slow; they're in love, floating in shafts of warm sun streaming through the swamp maples, kayaks tipping together as they embrace. They'll catch up later. How to find us? Just go with the flow.

We travel all morning through wooded swamp, drab, late-autumn banks splashed with the red fruits of winterberry holly. A few sprigs of it lend a Christmasy air to the kayaks' foredecks.

In a deep bend, protected from the wind that roars overhead like surf through the pine tops, we pass a bluff where I often come to reflect. I thought of some friends' recent loss of their child.

I had been searching for words to say to them. Maybe I'll bring them here in spring, when shad and herring and rockfish are thrusting up from the oceans to spawn, when shadbush and dogwood blossom on the banks and the maples are minting fresh green, payback for winter's skinflint wages.

Within yards of U.S. 50, a whitetail buck moves in on does by a wetland created when the new bridge at Vienna was built.

We can talk about how the only antidote to death is to celebrate renewal and life in all its forms. We'll plant a tree on the bank above the bend.

In camp that night, the river is wider, more powerful now. The fire warms our backs as sunset suffuses the water with pastels. Water laps the shoreline—her favorite music, a woman says.

Gifts of the river, subtle and unadvertised; ours for the taking, requiring only that we depart from our harried routines long enough to perceive them.

Late that night a tug inches past our camp, running lights shining like jewels against the far, dark shoreline. He runs this river two hundred times a year, the captain says quietly on the marine radio; never tires of it.

He's pushing upstream with a barge of Western Shore rock, returning with Delmarva sand. The full moon is making extra high tides, also extra low tides, exaggerating the Bay's inhalations and exhalations. The tug's engines strain to make four miles an hour, kayak pace, against the current. We'll break camp early to avoid battling the brunt of the incoming tide tomorrow.

In river time, the longest way is often best. By afternoon the tide has turned against us, but a friend and I, feeling robust, strike out across open water, shortcutting a big cove in a beeline for the next campsite. We thrash mightily against the shove of current.

Arriving, exhausted, we hear gentle splashing as a woman from our crew glides from the long, marshy, edge she'd followed round the cove, easily keeping pace out of the current, enjoying flights of quick-winged teal and noisy geese she startled from her path, also the solitary flaps of great blue herons.

That day we passed an eel potter, taking in his traps for the year, and bought some of his wrig-

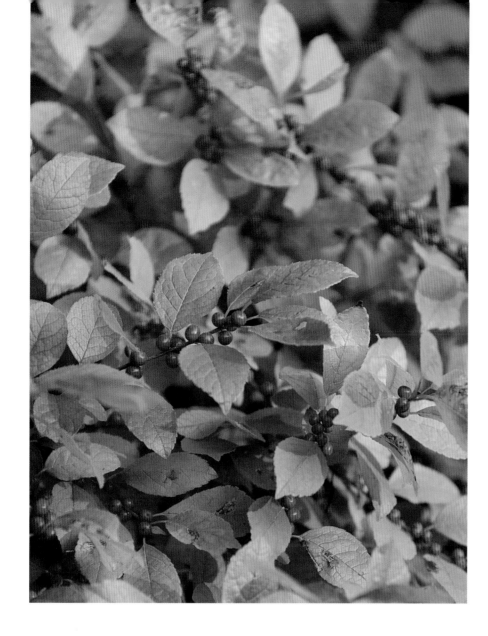

Winterberry holly shows its summer splendor.

gling catch—not my favorite dish, but it's what the river was offering.

Grilled in teriyaki sauce, it tastes fine that evening, and leads to a discussion about how every eel finds its way back to the Sargasso Sea to spawn. All of them die there, and how the young elvers make it back to repopulate every river and stream of the continent is far less understood than humans getting to the moon.

All these things and more the river offers— the sight of bald eagles, the taste of oysters, inspiration and reflection, turtles sunning on a log, light sparkling on wind-dimpled water; the cry of yellowlegs probing the mudflats to fuel their migration to Argentina, the wind singing in the pines, perch leaping in the moonlight just outside your tent.

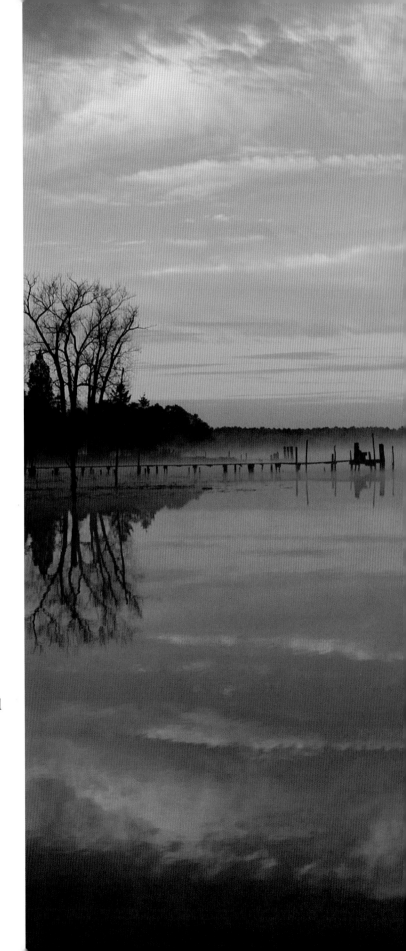

A perfect, calm morning reflects the pastels, mists, and forests of early April.

The nor'wester comes down hard the last day, propelling us downstream in a rush, overruling tides and currents. High overhead a glimmering string of tundra swans begins descending, arriving after a nonstop flight from the Canada–North Dakota border.

The river's gotten big down here, a mile wide, and it's a battle to stay upright as waves break on the deck. We turn into a protected marsh and wind our way to the haulout where the cars are parked. We're soaked and spent.

But not so fast. Sixty yards of sticky mud lie between us and landing. The north wind has blown the tide right out of the marshes, and we'll just have to wait a couple hours, watching hawks on the hunt soar and dip, and the play of light and breeze on the marsh's tawny pelt—gifts of the river, in river time.

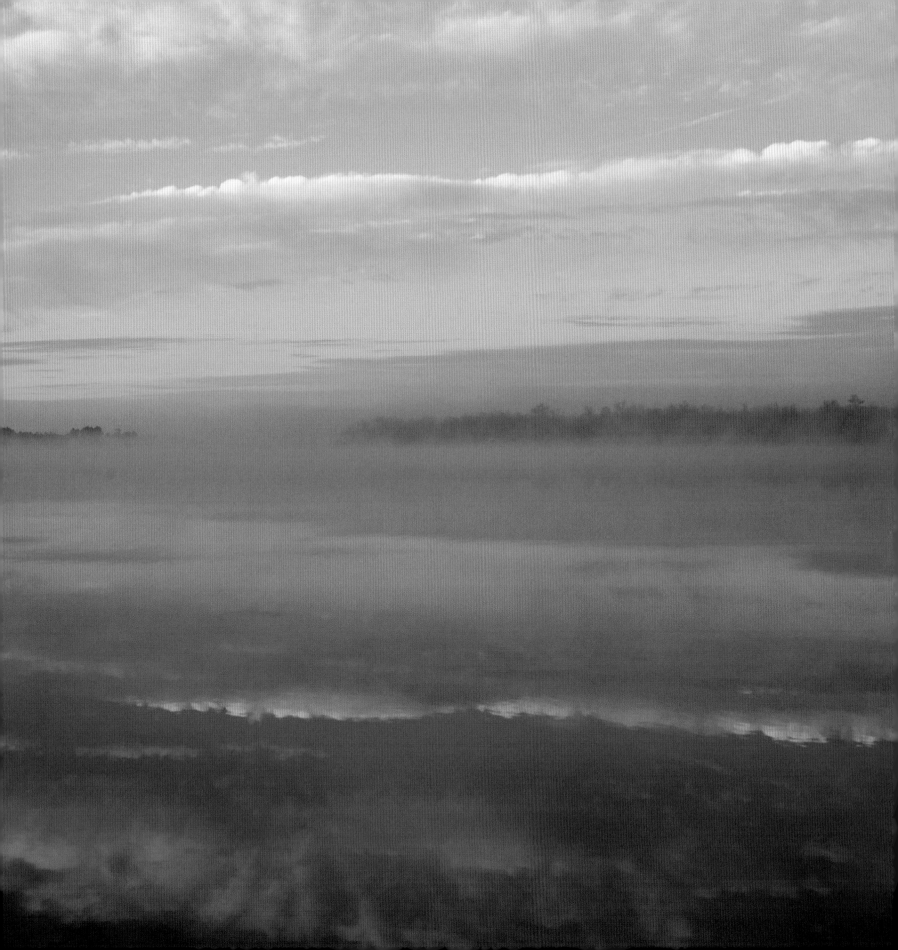

118

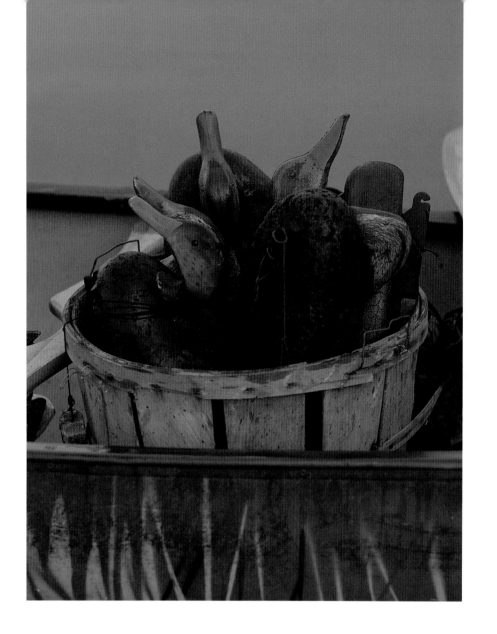

Opposite: Nanticoke folk:
Judith Stribling, president
of Friends of the Nanticoke,
and husband Dave Gooch
are avid duck hunters, paddling here on Wetipquin
Creek.

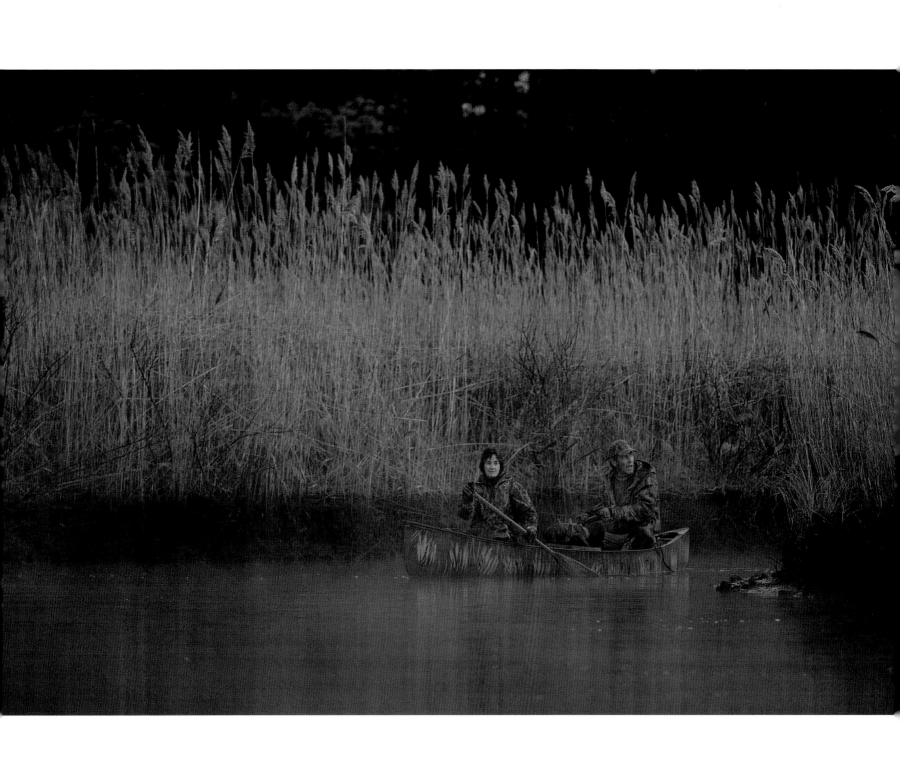

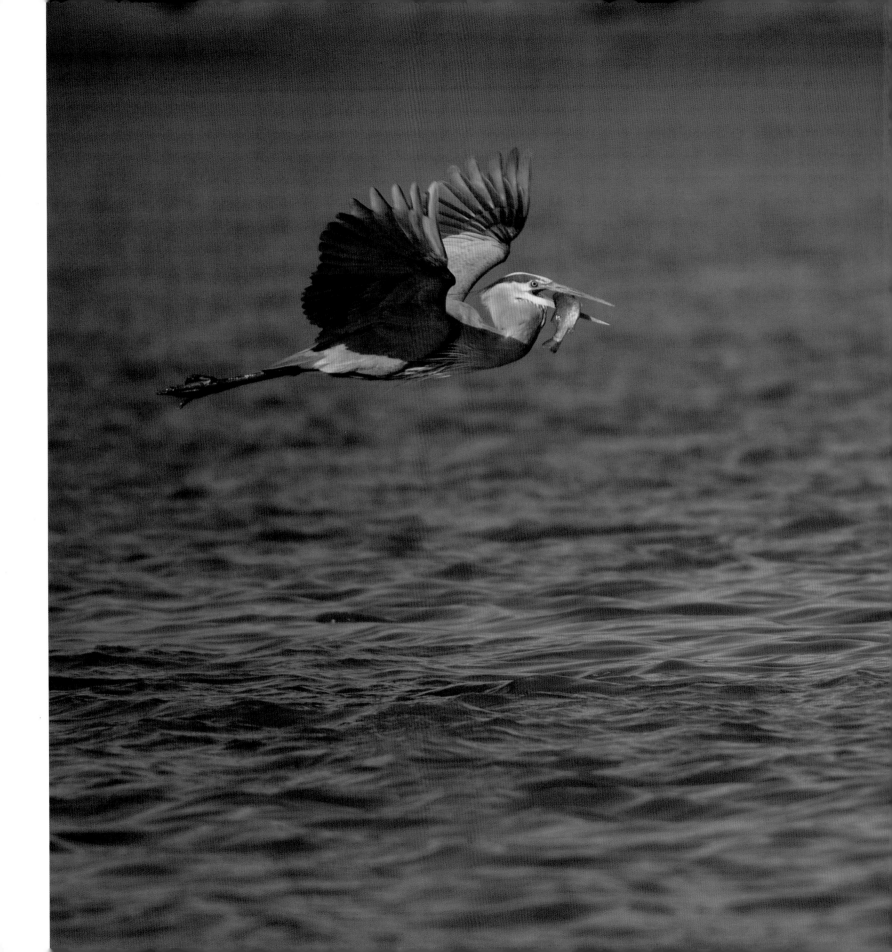

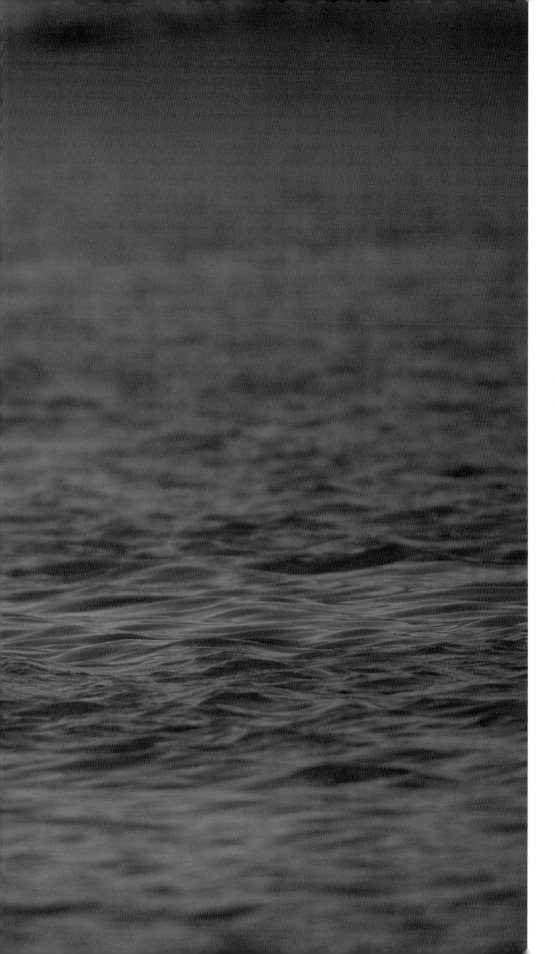

A great blue heron wings
off with a carryout meal,
a fish discarded by pound
netters.

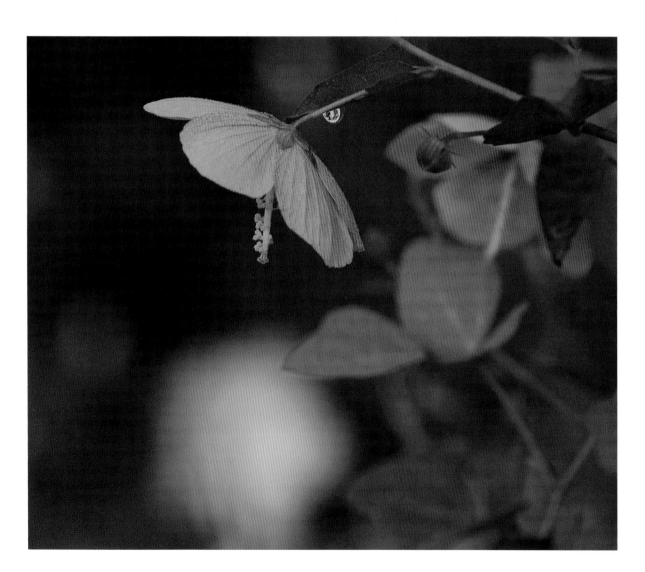

Pink mallows droop along a
mid-river wetland.

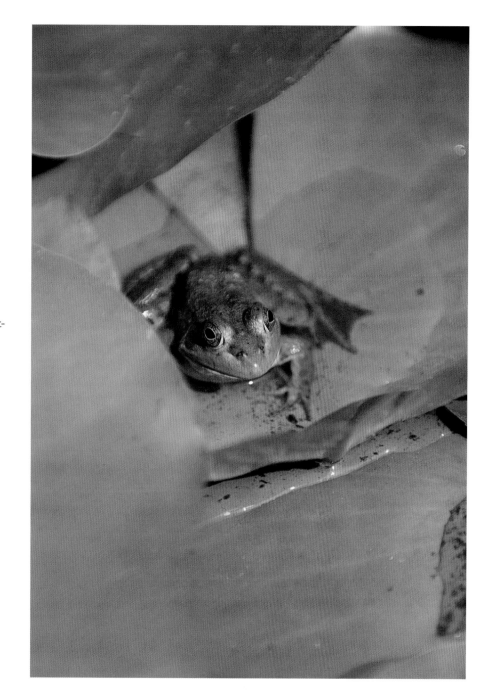

A green frog takes refuge on the broad leaf of a spatterdock.

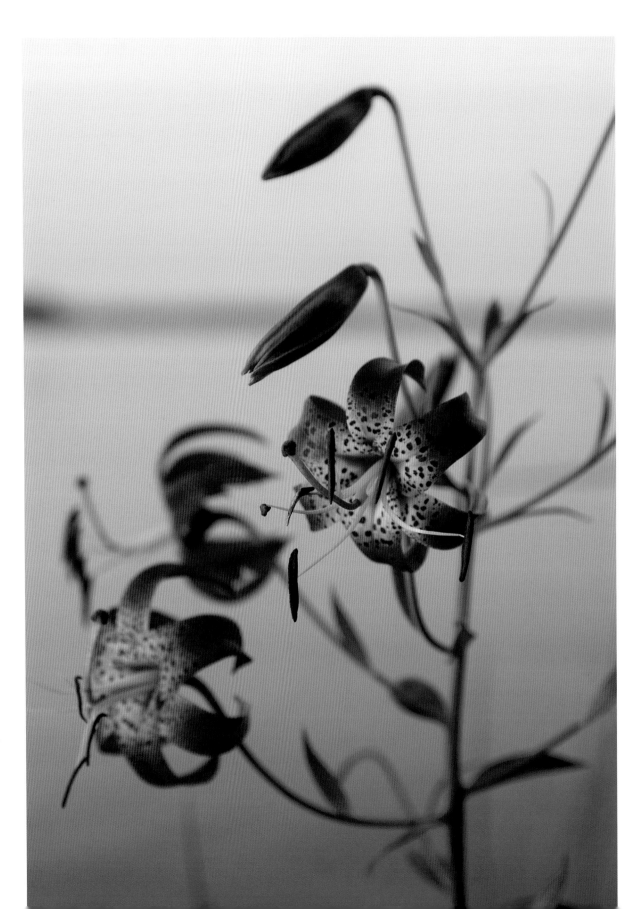

A Turk's Cap lily struts its stuff, enlivening the river's edge on an August afternoon.

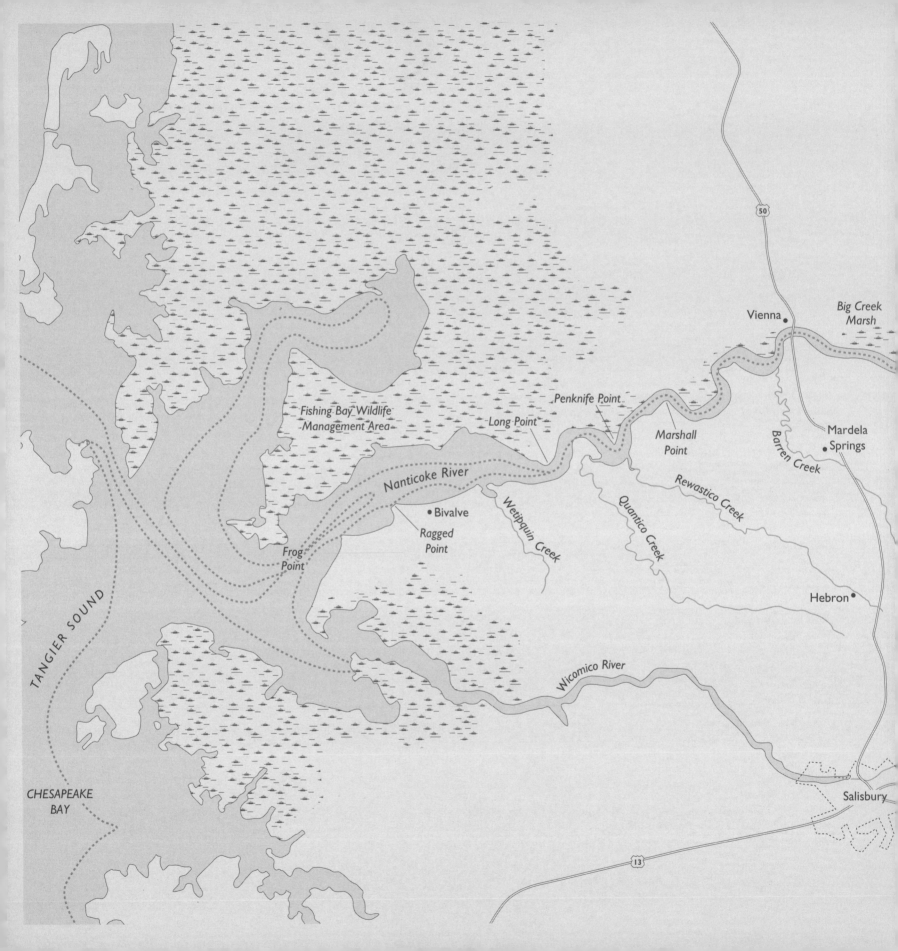

TANGIER SOUND

CHESAPEAKE
BAY

Fishing Bay Wildlife
Management Area

Nanticoke River

Frog
Point

Ragged
Point

•Bivalve

Long Point

Penknife Point

Marshall
Point

Wetipquin Creek

Quantico Creek

Rewastico Creek

Barren Creek

Wicomico River

Vienna

Big Creek
Marsh

Mardela
Springs

Hebron•

Salisbury

50

13